PENNY C. ROYAL

HERBALLY YOURS

1st Printing December 1976
2nd Printing January 1977
3rd Printing March 1977
4th Printing June 1977
5th Printing September 1977
6th Printing December 1977
7th Printing March 1978

BiWorld Publishers Inc.

P.O. Box 62 Provo, Utah 84601

Printed in the U.S.A. by

Microlith Printing Inc.

ISBN0-89557-012-2

TABLE OF CONTENTS

PREFACE

HERBALLY YOURS fills a demand for a comprehensive herbal handbook which is simplified enough for the beginning student and complete enough for the more advanced. It has an alphabetical list of Common Herbs, Health Problems, and some of the most popular Herbal Combinations being used today. There is a chapter on Diet and Cleansing; a brief section on Pregnancy, Nursing and Babies; and a list of Poisonous Herbs and Cautions. Also included is a chapter on Herbal Aid for Emergencies, and Directions on how to make and use herbal preparations such as poultices and tinctures. This book should answer most of your questions about natural health care for you and your family.

The author does not directly or indirectly dispense medical advice or prescribe the use of herbs as a form of treatment for sickness without medical approval. Nutritionists and other experts in the field of health and nutrition hold widely varying views. It is not the intent of the author to diagnose or prescribe. Our intent is only to offer health information to help you cooperate with your doctor in your mutual problem of building health. In the event you use this information without your doctor's approval, you are prescribing for yourself, which is your constitutional right, but the publisher assumes no responsibility.

Author
Penny C. Royal

INTRODUCTION

Dear Jan,

It was good to receive your letter, but I'm sorry you have had so many health problems. Your letter sounded so much like mine would have sounded several years ago. Perhaps if I share my story with you, it will give you comfort and encouragement.

Remember how carefree, energetic and full of life I was in college, and how I would eat anything I desired and never gain a pound? You always said, "Everyone has to watch their waistline, why don't you?"

Well, I took that same habit with me into my career. When most of the other employees had their roll and drink, I had to have creme pies and rich pastries. They were all so envious of me. But Jan, not one of them would envy me in the least had they seen me several years ago — it all caught up with me.

After receiving my immunization shots before going to Europe in 1962, I became very sick. I just assumed that everyone had the same reaction. By the time I arrived in France a month later, I was miserable and in so much pain, I literally could not carry my own purse.

After three months trying to ignore and bear the pain, I had to return home, only to find that my body was full of Rheumatoid Arthritis. This crippling disease is often brought on by stressful situations and settles in the weak areas of the body. In my case, the shots and foreign travel were more stress than my body could handle. It settled in my back, which was weak from a childhood injury. In any case, I was in pretty bad shape. This was the only time in my life I was considered "fat." I had gained 50 pounds and had that puffy, blown-up look.

After I returned home and received treatment from numerous doctors, and received very little encouragement, I decided I would just have to live with the pain. Since I was unable to return and teach school because of the frequent pain, and my inability to grasp a pencil or chalk, I finally got a job as a receptionist. I sat on a "donut pillow" with a heating pad at my back. It wasn't too bad as I fixed a fancy cover for my pillow and made a pocket in the back of my chair for the heating pad. In this manner I endured the situation while always seeking out any new doctor whom I thought might give me some relief.

About a year and a half later, I met my husband and we were married. When I started out with my first pregnancy, I had a very difficult time. I got Bell's palsy, then pneumonia, which lasted about two months. My delivery was very difficult. I didn't realize just how serious things were until I learned that the doctor slept just outside my room that first night. Also, I spent three days in the recovery room. It did seem rather strange that I had so many roommates during that time. Since the doctor wanted me to see my baby before I died, they brought her to me in the recovery room, which I learned later didn't happen too often. I had to have a blood transfusion and later realized this was when I got Hypoglycemia, or low blood sugar. At that time most doctors weren't too familiar with this disease. It wasn't generally known that diet had anything to do with that particular health problem. I continued to eat the sweets my body craved which gave me a temporary pick-up and when my sugar dropped, I'd just take another goodie. Little did I realize the damage I was causing to my adrenal glands and liver.

Some two years later, during my second pregnancy, I again got pneumonia and it lasted for 5 months. I had three doctors trying to figure out why my body rejected the antibiotics. They put me in and out of the hospital, but to no avail.

It was during this time that I had numerous problems with constipation and frequent pains in the colon area. The doctor diagnosed it as a nervous colon, then colitis, and finally diverticulitis. By this time, I knew things were getting pretty bad, so I made another appointment with a new clinic. At the end of six hours of testing and examinations by very competent internists, I was told that there was nothing very seriously wrong with me. I did have a slightly over-active thyroid, my blood was low, but in the normal range, I had a cyst on my ovary, but the doctor said it should be watched and possibly would go away without surgery. As for the pains in my colon, well, they wanted to do exploratory surgery and see what was going on inside. My strep throat was still a mystery. You can imagine how I felt as I left the clinic that day.

It was that night I walked the floor asking my Heavenly Father for help. I was guided to a lady who believed in herbs and diet and cleansing. I thought she was "something else," but since I had no other way to go, I followed her diet of raw juices. It was hard for me to suddenly give up all meat and animal products, and I didn't think I could ever exist without my sweets and pastries. I could have only fruits, vegetables, seeds and nuts. My body was so emaciated that it was very difficult to change so suddenly. I couldn't even think clearly — you know the feeling — fuzzy in the brain. I cried a lot and prayed more than I ever had. No one seemed to understand. My own family and friends ridiculed and teased me for the drastic change I had made in diet and cleansing. They knew I would be gone in a short time if I didn't get to a "good doctor." Thanks to an understanding husband, I was able to endure and keep trying. This lady gave me steam baths, and salt scrubs to try and open up my pores. She even gave me enemas to try and clean out the toxins from my system. You see, I didn't realize what I was doing to my body all of those years while I was enjoying my "junk food."

I finally reached the point, after three months, that I wanted to try things on my own. It was then that I got the flu and it really hit me hard. Now I realize that it could have been a cleanse that my body was experiencing. Somehow, I remembered a friend telling me about a masseur therapist who had helped her by suggesting only one herb. I had disregarded the story until I lay in bed so very ill. My husband called this therapist and after convincing him that I couldn't even make it to his office, he stopped by our home about 10:30 that evening. He put me on a coffee table in my living room and gave a massage that I shall never forget. Later he told me he never expected me to pull through the night, so he gave me everything he had. I was black and blue for some time after his treatment, but mighty greatful. Later, I learned that he didn't make house calls. I owe so much to this man, as he literally saved my life. He taught me how to use the herbs and how to live my diet.

I am so greatful for the health I now enjoy and the strength I have been blessed with, so I may in return help others. Even though I still experience bad days, the good ones are more numerous, and the bad ones less frequent. I realize that the body has to back track in order to heal, and the more I study, the more of a miracle I feel it is.

I no longer crave sweets, my body seems to crave things that are good and healthy. I even like vegetables that I didn't even know existed. We keep our meals simple and eat half as much and feel twice as good. I'm so greatful that my husband and children have accepted this change. Oh, I still cheat occasionally, but not too often because I end up paying for it.

Jan, I am no doctor and I can't prescribe or diagnose, but when you reach a point that your body rejects antibiotics, you learn other ways. Please accept the things I have learned and I know you too can experience good health once again.

Since I detest the taste of herb tea, I have had the most experience with capsulated herbs. That doesn't necessarily mean that they are the best, but I found that if I drink plenty of water with them, I get fantastic results. I also know that certain combinations of herbs help specific problems. One person may utilize three out of six while another may use three different ones.

Herbs were put here for our use and I would like to share with you several of my favorite scriptures which kept me encouraged in my search for health.

Genesis 1:29- 30

"And God said, Behold, I have given you every herb bearing seed, which is upon the face of all the earth, and every tree, in the which is the fruit of a tree yielding seed; to you it shall be for meat.

"And to every beast of the earth, and to every fowl of the air, and to everything that creepeth upon the earth, wherein there is life, I have given every green herb for meat: and it was so."

Doctrine & Covenants, Section 89:10-11

"And again, verily I say unto you, all wholesome herbs God hath ordained for the constitution, nature, and use of man —

"Every herb in the season thereof, and every fruit in the season thereof; all these to be used with prudence and thanksgiving."

Doctrine & Covenants, Section 42:43

"And whosoever among you are sick, and have not faith to be healed, but believe, shall be nourished with all tenderness, with herbs and mild food, and that not by the hand of an enemy."

Anyone who is sincerely searching can learn just what is best for his body and in what quantity. And now, after changing my way of life, I no longer suffer from Arthritis, Migraine Headaches, or Strep Throat. My Hypoglycemia is under control, only occasionally do I suffer from Hemorrhoids. I haven't had Pneumonia for several years.It is wonderful to think clearly once again. I enjoy being alive!

Now, Jan, knowing how much it will mean to you, I dedicate this book to you and many others who are sincerely searching for health, vitality, and a new way of life — through proper diet, herbs, rest, exercise, cleansing, good water, and a healthy mental attitude — and to all of those who have devoted their life to helping others.

HERBALLY YOURS

PENNY C. ROYAL

Chapter 1

DEFINITIONS AND DIRECTIONS

The author does not directly or indirectly dispense medical advice or prescribe the use of herbs as a form of treatment for sickness without medical approval. Nutritionists and other experts in the field of health and nutrition hold widely varying views. It is not the intent of the author to diagnose or prescribe. Our intent is only to offer health information to help you cooperate with your doctor in your mutual problem of building health. In the event you use this information without your doctor's approval, you are prescribing for yourself, which is your constitutional right, but the publisher assumes no responsibility.

DECOCTION:
A tea made of the roots and bark.
Use 1 Tablespoon of the cut herb or 1 teaspoon of the powdered herb. Gently boil in one cup of water for 30 minutes. Let stand 10 minutes.

FOMENTATION:
A cloth wrung out of hot infusion or decoction and applied to the affected area. This is usually not as effective as a poultice.

INFUSION:
A tea made of the leaves and blossoms.
Use 1 teaspoon of the powdered herb. Bring 1 cup of water to boiling. Remove from heat. Add the herb. Cover and steep for 10 minutes.

OIL OF HERBS:
An extraction of the herb in an oil base.
Place the powdered herb in the top of a double boiler. Cover with olive oil. Cook on low heat for 3 to 3½ hours. Extract the oil from the mixture. Bottle in dark glass bottles.

POULTICE:	*A moist, hot herb pack applied locally.* If using the fresh herb, crush and bruise it. The powdered herb may be used also. Mix with mineral water (or other liquid) to form a thick paste. Spread on a clean cloth and cover the affected area. Leave on for several hours. Always use a fresh poultice. Never re-heat to use over.
TINCTURE:	*An extraction of herbs in vinegar or alcohol.* Apple Cider Vinegar is all right for most herbal tinctures. If the herb is oily or sticky, Everclear Brand 190 Proof can be used successfully.

COMMON POULTICES

Fresh:	Crush the fresh herb and mix with enough water to make a thick paste, apply to affected area. Put cloth over wound. Change as it dries out. (Plastic may be used to hold moisture in.)
Dried:	Mix herb with cornmeal or flaxseed to make thick paste. Add enough boiling water to hold together. Spread on cloth and apply to affected area. Cover and use plastic to hold in moisture.
BAYBERRY	*Cancerous sores, Ulcerated sores.*
COMFREY	*Burns, Sprains, Wounds.*
LOBELIA and MULLEIN	*Lumps, Lymph Congestion, Swellings.* 1 part Lobelia to 3 parts Mullein.
LOBELIA and SLIPPERY ELM	*Abcesses, Bites, Blood Poisoning, Boils, Rheumatism, Wounds.* 1/3 part Lobelia to 2/3 parts Slippery Elm.
ONION	*Boils, Sores, Tonsillitis, Ears, Infection* Use the whole onion which has been heated in oven for earache. Place in against ear to help

8

draw infection out. The onion should be chopped and heated for poultice.

(24)   *Boils, Burns, Cuts, Wounds.*
Mix herbs with either vitamin E or mineral water to make paste. Apply vitamin E on wound before applying paste. Change daily.

PLANTAIN   *Blood Poisoning, Dog Bites.*

POKE ROOT   *Caked Breasts.*

POTATO   *Growths, Infection, Tumors.*
Grate a raw red potato and add 1 teaspoon ginger. Can be used for internal cysts also.

SLIPPERY ELM   *Sores, Wounds, Pleurisy*
Excellent mixed with other herbs.

COMMON TINCTURES

ANTISPASMODIC   Place herbs in 1 quart of Brandy.

    1 oz. Lobelia
    1 oz. Scullcap
    1 oz. Skunk Cabbage
    1 oz. Myrrh
    1 oz. Black Cohosh
    ½ oz. Cayenne

B & B   Place herbs in 1 pint 190 proof alcohol.

    1 oz. Black Cohosh
    1 oz. Blue Cohosh
    1 oz. Blue Vervain
    1 oz. Lobelia
    1 oz. Scullcap

Use for earache, epilepsy, hiccoughs, and muscle spasms.

LOBELIA   Place in 1 pint Apple Cider Vinegar.

    4 oz. Lobelia

9

Add the herbs to the vinegar or alcohol. Let set for 14 days, shaking 2 or 3 times each day. On the 14th day strain and filter it. If left longer it goes weak. Place in dark glass bottles.

GREEN DRINK

A cleansing, nutritious drink made from herbs, is what we call the "green drink." Many herbs can be used, but we find that if you use no more than four at a time it tastes better. Here are a few ideas for the drink.

Put fresh Pineapple or unsweetened Pineapple Juice in the blender then add any of the following:

Burdock, Carrot tops, **Celery**, Chard, **Comfrey**, Dandelion, Marshmallow, **Parsley**, Plantain, Radish tops, Raspberry Leaves, Sprouts, Wheat Grass.

Blend and strain. Make fresh each day.

CAUTION: Do not use Potato Leaves or Rhubarb Leaves.

Chapter 2

COMMON HERBS

The herbs are used in capsules or teas unless otherwise indicated. The words in bold type are the ones with which we have had the most experience.

ALFALFA

Allergies
Anemia
Appetite
Arthritis
Bad Breath
Blood Purifier
Bursitis

Cramps
Diabetes
Digestion
Gout
Kidneys
Morning Sickness
Nausea

Pituitary Gland
Rheumatism
Stomach
Teeth
Ulcers

Alfalfa is deep rooted and it picks up the **trace minerals** in the soil. It also contains the eight **digestive enzymes** and the eight essential **amino acids** of protein. It is very rich in **vitamins** and **minerals** including Vitamin U for peptic ulcers.

ALOE VERA

Abrasions
Acne
Athlete's Foot
Burns
Constipation

Ear Infection
Eczema
Fever Blisters
Hair Growth
Hemorrhoids

Mouth Sores
Poison Ivy
Poison Oak
Psoriasis
Ulcerated Sores

BARBERRY (ROCKY MOUNTAIN GRAPE, WILD OREGON GRAPE)

Anemia
Bladder
Blood Purifier
Boils

Constipation
Diarrhea
Digestion
Gall Bladder

Gall Stones
Gums
Heart
Heartburn

High Blood Pressure	Mouthwash	Throat
Jaundice	Rheumatism	Vagina
Kidney	Skin Diseases	
Liver	Spleen	

Barberry improves the appetite by promoting bile secretion. It will help eliminate gas when used with one part Wild Yam. It has also been used for High Blood Pressure as it dilates the blood vessels.

BAYBERRY

Canker	Hay Fever	Prolapsed Uterus
Chills	Hemorrhage	Scarlet Fever
Colds	Hoarseness	Sinus
Colon	Indigestion	Stomach
Cuts	Leucorrhea	Throat
Diarrhea	Lumbago	Thyroid
Digestion	Lungs	Ulcers
Dysentery	Menstruation	Varicose Veins
Eyes	Miscarriage	**Wounds**
Gargle	**Mucous Membrane**	

BISTORT

| Bed Wetting | Bites | Menstruation |
| **Bleeding** | Diarrhea | Vagina |

Bistort has been used as a mouthwash for gum problems or inflammation of the mouth.

BLACK COHOSH

Arthritis	**Hormone Balance**	Pulse
Asthma	High Blood Pressure	Rheumatism
Bee Stings	**Hot Flashes**	Skin Disease
Bites	Kidneys	Smoking
Blood Purifier	Liver	Snake Bites
Bronchitis	Lumbago	St. Vitus Dance
Coughs	Lungs	Thyroid
Diabetes	**Menopause**	Uterus
Diarrhea	**Menstruation**	
Epilepsy	Nerves	
Headaches	Paralysis	

Black Cohosh is a natural supplier of **Estrogen**. If headaches occur while taking this herb, the body probably has sufficient estrogen and therefore the herb is not needed.

BLACK WALNUT

Boils	Leucorrhea	Syphillis
Diarrhea	Lupus	Teeth
Eczema	**Parasites**	Vagina
Herpes	Poison Ivy	
Lactation	**Ringworm**	

Black Walnut has been used successfully in a tincture for Poison Ivy, Ringworm, and other types of skin disorders. It may also be used as a poultice or taken internally.

A powder may be used in brushing teeth to help restore the enamel.

BLESSED THISTLE

Appetite	Fever	Indigestion
Arthritis	Gall Bladder	Kidneys
Constipation	Gas	Leucorrhea
Cramps	**Hormone Balance**	Lungs
Digestion	Headache	Migraine Headaches

It has been used to increase the milk in **nursing** mothers, and also to make the milk richer.

BLACK WILLOW (See WILLOW)

BLUE COHOSH

Bladder Infection	Convulsions	Heart
Blood Pressure	**Cramps**	Kidneys
Blood Purifier	Diabetes	Leucorrhea
Childbirth	Diuretic	**Menstruation**
Colic	Epilepsy	Spasms

Blue Cohosh has been used for years by the Indians to make Childbirth easier. If the baby is ready to be born, it has been known to help dilate the Cervix, thus making the delivery easier.

BRIGHAM TEA (DESERT TEA, MORMON TEA, SQUAW TEA)

Arthritis	Fever	Rheumatism
Asthma	Headaches	Scarlet Fever
Blood Pressure	Kidney Disorders	Skin Eruptions
Blood Purifier	Menstruation	Sinus
Colds	Nose Bleeds	

For nose bleeds and sinus problems, the tea is snuffed up the nose.
CAUTION: Brigham Tea can increase nervousness and restlessness.

BUCHU

Bed Wetting	Gravel	Rheumatism
Bladder Weakness	Pancreas	Uretheral Irritation
Diabetes	Prostate	Venereal Disease

BUCKTHORN

Constipation	Itching	**Skin Diseases**
Gall Stones	Liver	Warts
Gout	Parasites	
Hemorrhoids	Rheumatism	

BURDOCK

Acne	**Cleansing**	Nerves
Allergies	**Eczema**	Obesity
Arthritis	Endurance	Poison Ivy and Oak
Baldness	Gall Bladder	Psoriasis
Bladder	Gall Stones	Rheumatism
Blood Purifier	Gout	**Skin Diseases**
Boils	Hay Fever	Stomach
Burns	Hemorrhoids	Throat
Bursitis	Itching	Ulcers
Cankers	Kidneys	Venereal Disease
Chicken Pox	Liver	

Burdock helps to reduce **swelling** and deposits in **joints**. It also helps
to regulate the urine flow.

CAMOMILE

Appetite	Bladder	Bronchitis
Asthma	Bleeding	Callouses
Bowels	Blood Purifier	Corns

14

Colds	Gangrene	Measles
Colitis	Gas	Menstruation
Cramps	Headache	Nerves
Dandruff	Hemorrhoids	**Parasites**
Diverticulitis	Hysteria	Pain
Dizziness	Indigestion	Spleen
Drug Withdrawal	Jaundice	Stomach
Eyes	Kidneys	Swelling

It has been used successfully as a cleanser for those who have used **drugs** over a long period of time.

CAPSICUM (See CAYENNE)

CAROB (St. JOHNS BREAD)

Colitis	Digestion	Stomach
Diarrhea		

CASCARA SAGRADA

Colon	**Gall Bladder**	Jaundice
Constipation	Gall Stones	**Liver**
Cough	Hemorrhoids	Nerves
Croup	Indigestion	Spleen
Digestion	Intestines	

Cascara Sagrada is good if taken upon retiring as it helps to relax and soothe.

CATNIP

Bronchitis	Hypoglycemia	**Nerves**
Colds	Hysteria	Nightmares
Colic	Insanity	Pain
Contagious Diseases	Insomnia	Parasites
Diarrhea	Kidney Stones	Smoking
Dizziness	**Measles**	Stress
Fever	Menstruation	**Tension**
Gas	Miscarriage	Urination
Headache	Morning Sickness	Uterus

To help bring down a fever, use 1 Tablespoon of Catnip to one quart of water. Make as a tea and strain. Cool to tepid and use in enema.

This enema is soothing and relaxing and will help bring the fever down by dislodging the congestion.

CAYENNE (CAPSICUM)

Acne	Diabetes	Pancreas
Appetite	Digestion	Paralysis
Arthritis	Endurance	Parkinson's Disease
Arteriosclerosis	Energy	Pleurisy
Asthma	Eyes	Pyorrhea
Bleeding	Fatigue	Rheumatism
Blood Pressure	Gas	**Shock**
Bronchitis	Hangovers	Spleen
Chills	Hay Fever	Sprains
Circulation	**Heart**	Stomach
Colds	Indigestion	Throat
Contagious Diseases	Infection	Vagina
Convulsions	Jaundice	Varicose Veins
Coughs	Kidneys	Wounds
Cramps	Lockjaw	
Cuts	Palsy	

Cayenne has been recognized as one of the greatest of all herbs and foods not only for the **entire digestive system**, but for the circulatory system as well. It has been known to be an excellent remedy for Hemorrhoids. It helps to regulate the heart and strengthen the pulse rate while it cleanses the **circulatory system**.

When taken with Ginger, it helps clean out the bronchial tubes. When it is used with other herbs, it acts as a catalyst and increases the effectiveness of the other herbs. It is used for those who are in shock. Cayenne also helps stop internal or external bleeding if taken internally, or if the wound is small, Cayenne may be applied directly to it.

CHAPARRAL

Acne	Cataracts	Prostate
Allergies	Cramps	**Psoriasis**
Arthritis	Eyesight	Rheumatism
Blood Purifier	Hair Growth	Tumors
Boils	Hay Fever	Warts
Bursitis	Kidneys	
Cancer	Obesity	

CHICKWEED

Acne
Allergies
Appetite
Asthma
Blood Poisoning
Boils
Bowels
Bronchitis
Burns
Cancer
Canker
Circulation
Cleanser
Constipation
Diabetes
Hay Fever
Hemorrhoids
Hoarseness
Itching
Impotency
Lungs
Mouth Sores
Obesity
Pleurisy
Psoriasis
Rheumatism
Skin Problems
Stomach
Throat
Tumors
Wounds

COMFREY

Allergies
Anemia
Arthritis
Asthma
Bites
Bladder
Bleeding
Blood Purifier
Boils
Bronchitis
Bruises
Burns
Bursitis
Colitis
Colon
Coughs
Cramps
Diabetes
Diarrhea
Digestion
Eczema
Emphysema
Fatigue
Fractures
Gall Bladder
Gout
Gums
Hay Fever
Hoarseness
Indigestion
Infection
Inflammation
Kidneys
Leucorrhea
Lungs
Menstruation
Mucous Membranes
Pancreas
Psoriasis
Rheumatism
Sprains
Stomach
Swellings
Throat
Tonsillitis
Ulcers

DAMIANA

Female Problems
Frigidity
Hormones
Hot Flashes
Menopause
Parkinson's Disease
Prostate
Sex Stimulant

Damiana is recognized as being good for females generally, and helps to balance female hormones.

DANDELION

Acne	Diabetes	Jaundice
Age Spots	Eczema	Kidneys
Anemia	Endurance	**Liver**
Appetite	Energy	**Low Blood Pressure**
Bladder	Fatigue	Pancreas
Blood Purifier	Fever	Psoriasis
Boils	Gall Bladder	Senility
Bronchitis	Gall Stones	Skin Diseases
Cancer	Hemorrhage	Spleen
Cleansing	Hypoglycemia	Vitality
Constipation	Indigestion	Wounds
Cramps	Insomnia	

Dandelion contains organic sodium and is very good for **anemia**, caused by a deficiency of nutritive salts, and is recognized as a great **blood builder** and purifier. It is also effective as a liver cleanser. It is very high in calcium and other nutrients.

ECHINACEA

Acne	Boils	Lymph
Bad Breath	Carbuncles	Prostate
Bee Stings	Fever	Smoking
Bites	Gangrene	Snake Bites
Bladder Infection	Gums	Tonsillitis
Blood Poisoning	Hemorrhage	Venereal Disease
Blood Purifier	**Infection**	Wounds

It has been known to cleanse the blood in gangrene conditions. It is especially good for congestion of the **lymphatic system** and glands. It is often used with Myrrh.

EUCALYPTUS

Bronchitis	Croup	**Lungs**
Cancer	Fever	Paralysis

EYEBRIGHT

Allergies	Diabetes	**Hay Fever**
Cataracts	Digestion	

Eyebright has been used for all kinds of **Eye Ailments** and has been known to strengthen the eyes and improve the eyesight. The tea may be used as an eye wash or the herb may be taken internally.

FALSE UNICORN

Diabetes	Menstruation	Uterus
Hemorrhage	**Miscarriage**	Vagina
Leucorrhea	Prolapsed Uterus	
Longevity	**Sterility**	

It strengthens the muscles of the uterus and has been used for all types of complications of pregnancy.

FENNEL

Appetite	Emphysema	Menstruation
Bed Wetting	Eye Wash	Migraine Headaches
Bites	Gall Bladder	Mucous
Bronchitis	**Gas**	Obesity
Colic	Gout	Rheumatism
Convulsions	Hoarseness	Sinus
Coughs	**Indigestion**	Spasms
Cramps	Jaundice	Urination

Fennel helps to increase milk for nursing mothers.

FENUGREEK

Allergies	Eyes	**Mucous Membranes**
Anemia	Fever	Stomach
Bronchitis	Frigidity	Throat
Bruises	Hay Fever	Vagina
Coughs	**Heartburn**	Voice
Diabetes	**Hoarseness**	Water Retention
Digestion	Lungs	
Emphysema	**Migraine Headaches**	

Fenugreek is an intestinal lubricant and is healing for sores and ulcers in the intestines.

GARLIC

Appetite	Arteriosclerosis	**Blood Pressure**

Cancer	Gall Bladder	Rabies
Contagious Diseases	**Gas**	Rheumatism
Coughs	Heart	Sinus
Cramps	**High Blood Pressure**	Stomach
Diarrhea	Indigestion	Ulcers
Diverticulitis	Liver	Vagina
Emphysema	**Parasites**	Warts
Fever	Prostate	**Yeast Infection**

Garlic acts as a **natural antibiotic**, destroying only the harmful bacteria. The good bacteria are left alone to help fight the illness. For yeast infection, blend one clove of fresh garlic in one pint of water. Strain. Add one more pint of water and use as a douche. Where fresh Garlic is not available, one or two capsules of garlic and cayenne may be opened and added to one quart of water. (Use as a douche.)

GENTIAN

Appetite	Gout	Liver
Gas		

GINGER

Bronchitis	Diarrhea	Mumps
Colds	**Digestion**	Nausea
Colon Spasms	Endurance	Paralysis
Colitis	Flu	Pneumonia
Constipation	**Gas**	Shock
Chicken Pox	Headache	Sinus
Contagious Diseases	Hemorrhage	Stomach Spasms
Coughs	Menstruation	Vagina
Cramps	**Morning Sickness**	

By adding three or four Tablespoons to the **bath** water, Ginger will help open the skin pores. This will help get rid of excess waste. It is very effective for colds and flu.
Ginger is especially good for colon gas when taken before each meal.

GINSENG

Acne	**Appetite**	Cancer
Age Spots	Asthma	Colds
Aging	Bleeding	Constipation

Convulsions	**Frigidity**	Prostate
Coughs	Gas	Regulates Hormones
Digestion	Inflammation	Stomach
Endurance	**Longevity**	Strength
Energy	Lungs	Whooping Cough
Fever	Parkinson's Disease	

Ginseng helps to regulate the male hormones when used with Sarsaparilla. According to studies done in Russia, the high level of physical, spiritual, emotional, and mental endurance has been attributed to the widespread use of Ginseng.

GOLDEN SEAL

Alcoholism	**Hemorrhage**	Prostate
Allergies	Hemorrhoids	Psoriasis
Appetite	Hoarseness	Pyorrhea
Asthma	Indigestion	Ringworm
Bad Breath	***Infection**	Scarlet Fever
Bladder	Inflammation	Sinus
Bronchitis	Itching	Skin Cancer
Burns	Kidneys	Skin Disease
Cankers	Leucorrhea	Spleen
Chicken Pox	Liver	Stomach
Circulation	Lymph	Sores
Colds	Measles	Throat
Colitis	Menstruation	Thyroid
Constipation	Morning Sickness	Tonsillitis
Diabetes	Mucous Membranes	Ulcers
Digestion	Mouth Sores	Urethra
Eye Wash	Mouthwash	Uterus
Eczema	Nasal Passages	Vagina
Flu	Nausea	Venereal Disease
Gall Bladder	Nerves	Water Retention
Gums	**Nose Bleeds**	**Wounds**
Hay Fever	Obesity	
Heart	Pancreas	

*If a person has Hypoglycemia, Myrrh may be used in place of Golden Seal as Golden Seal tends to lower the blood sugar level.

GOTU KOLA

Aging	**Age Spots**	High Blood Pressure

Brain Food	**Memory**	Senility
Energy	Menopause	Vitality
Endurance	**Mental Fatigue**	
Longevity	**Pituitary**	

GRAVEL ROOT (See QUEEN OF THE MEADOW)

HAWTHORN

Arteriosclerosis	Endurance	Low Blood Pressure
Arthritis	**Energy**	Menopause
Blood Pressure	Heart	Rheumatism
Emotional Stress	Insomnia	

Hawthorn can produce dizziness if taken in too large of doses.

HOPS

Appetite	**Insomnia**	Obesity
Bedwetting	Jaundice	Parasites
Coughs	Liver	Rheumatism
Earaches	Menstruation	Sex Desire
Fever	Morning Sickness	Toothache
Headaches	**Nerves**	Ulcers
Hoarseness	Nightmares	Water Retention
Indigestion	**Night Sweats**	

HORSERADISH

Appetite	Digestion	Rheumatism
Arthritis	Gout	Sciatica
Asthma	Hoarseness	**Sinus**
Bladder	Lungs	Skin
Circulation	Mucous Membranes	Water Retention
Coughs	Parasites	Wounds

Horseradish will clear **nasal passages** in nursing babies. Cut the fresh herb and let the baby smell the fumes. It is also good for swollen Liver and Spleen.

HORSETAIL

| Baldness | Convulsions | Diuretic |
| Bleeding | Diabetes | Eyes |

Feet	Jaundice	Nerves
Heart	Liver	
Hemorrhage	Mucous	

Because of the high Silica content, it builds strong **fingernails** and helps split ends on the **hair**.

HYSSOP

Asthma	Digestion	Measles
Bee Stings	Eyes	Mucous Membranes
Bites	Gas	Night Sweats
Bladder	Gall Bladder	Parasites
Blood Purifier	Gall Stones	Perspiration
Blood Pressure	Hoarseness	Seizures
Bruises	Inflammation	Sinus
Burns	Intestines	Skin
Circulation	Kidneys	Toothache
Convulsions	Lice	Throat
Cough	Liver	Ulcers
Diarrhea	Lungs	

For Toothache, boil the herb in vinegar and rinse the mouth with it.

IRISH MOSS

Bad Breath	Cough	Pneumonia
Cancer	Jaundice	**Thyroid**
Convulsions	**Obesity**	

JOJOBA

| Baldness | Hair Loss | Seborrhea |
| Dandruff | Psoriasis | |

JUNIPER

Adrenal	Blood	Kidneys
Allergies	Boils	Lumbago
Appetite	Coughs	Mucous
Arthritis	**Diabetes**	**Pancreas**
Baldness	Diuretic	Prostate
Bed Wetting	Dog Bites	Stomach
Bee Stings	Gas	Throat
Bites	Hay Fever	Water Retention
Bladder	**Hypoglycemia**	

23

Excellent for prevention of disease. Tea of berries can be used on Insect Bites, Bee Stings, and Dog Bites.

KELP

Adrenal	Diabetes	**Pituitary**
Anemia	Eczema	Pregnancy
Birth Defects	Goiter	Prostate
Bursitis	Hot Flashes	Psoriasis
Childbirth	Kidneys	**Thyroid**
Colitis	Menopause	Weight Distribution
Cramps (leg)	Morning Sickness	

LICORICE

Addison's Disease	Cushing's Disease	Menopause
Age Spots	**Drug Withdrawal**	Sex Stimulant
Arthritis	Emphysema	Stomach
Asthma	**Endurance**	Throat
Blood Purifier	**Female Complaints**	Tonic
Bronchitis	Hoarseness	Ulcers
Colds	**Hypoglycemia**	**Vitality**
Constipation	Longevity	
Coughs	Lungs	

Contains **Natural Hormones.**

LOBELIA

Allergies	**Ear Infection**	**Miscarriage**
Arthritis	Fevers	Mucous Membranes
Asthma	Hay Fever	**Nerves**
Bites	Headache	**Pain**
Boils	Heart Palpitations	Palsy
Bronchitis	Hoarseness	Pleurisy
Bruises	**Hyperactivity**	**Pneumonia**
Bursitis	**Hypoglycemia**	**Poisoning (food)**
Chicken Pox	Hysteria	Poison Ivy
Congestion	Indigestion	Poultice
Contagious Diseases	Insanity	Rabies
Convulsions	Jaundice	**Relaxant**
Coughs	Liver	Rheumatic Fever
Croup	**Lock Jaw**	Rheumatism
Digestion	**Lungs**	Ringworm
Earache	Migraine Headaches	Scarlet Fever

Shock	Tetanus	Wounds
St. Vitus Dance	Toothache	
Teething	Tumors	

Should be used with Cayenne or Peppermint (or another stimulant). Lobelia is very relaxing if taken in small doses, it will cause vomiting if large doses are given. Tincture of Lobelia should be used for the following: Croup, Asthma, Earache, Lock Jaw, and Ringworm.

MAGNOLIA

| Fever | Smoking | Vagina |

MANDRAKE

Colitis	Gall Bladder	Warts
Constipation	Gall Stones	
Fever	Liver	

MARSHMALLOW

Allergies	Emphysema	Laryngitis
Asthma	Eye Wash	**Lungs**
Bed Wetting	Flu	Mucous Membranes
Bladder	Hay Fever	Nerves
Bleeding (Urinary)	Hoarseness	Pain
Burns	Inflammation	Pneumonia
Coughs	**Kidneys**	Throat
Diabetes	Lactation	Vaginal Irritation

To bring in rich milk in **nursing mothers,** take as a warm tea.

MISTLETOE

Convulsions	**Hemorrhage**	Hysteria
Gall Bladder	High Blood Pressure	**Menstruation**
Heart	Hypoglycemia	Nerves

CAUTION: May cause vomiting if taken in large doses. Use with caution only if other herbs don't work.

MULLEIN

| **Asthma** | **Bronchitis** | Constipation |
| Boils | Bruises | Coughs |

25

Croup	**Hemorrhage**	Skin Disease
Diarrhea	**(Bowel, Lungs)**	Throat
Diaper Rash	Mucous Membranes	Toothaches
Earaches	Mumps	Tumors
Eyes	Pleurisy	Warts
Frostbite	Pneumonia	Whooping Cough
Glands (Swollen)	Poison Ivy	
Hay Fever	**Sinus**	

Use leaves to make a tea for Asthma. Flowers steeped in oil is a good ointment for Bruises and **Frostbite**.

MYRRH

Asthma	Indigestion	Teeth (Stained)
Bad Breath	Infection	Throat Sores
Boils	Leucorrhea	Thrush
Cankers	Lungs	Thyroid
Colitis	Menstruation	Toothache
Colon	**Mouth Sores**	Ulcers
Coughs	Nerves	Uterus
Cuts	Scarlet Fever	Vagina
Douche	Shock	Wounds
Gums	Stomach	

In Emergency Childbirth it can be applied to the naval after the cord is removed. It will help heal and prevent **infection**. For throat and mouth sores, use as a gargle and mouthwash.

NETTLE

Baldness	Boils	Stomach
Bleeding	Night Sweat	Urinary Tract

OAT STRAW

Appetite	Frostbite	Liver
Arthritis	Gall Bladder	Lumbago
Bed Wetting	Gout	Lungs
Bladder	Gravel	**Nerves**
Boils	Heart	Paralysis
Bursitis	Jaundice	**Rheumatism**
Eyes	Kidneys	

PAPAYA

Allergies	Gas	Stomach
Digestion	Hemorrhage	Worms
Diverticulitis	Paralysis	Wounds

Contains Papain which is an enzyme similar to pepsin — one produced by the stomach. Papaya can be mixed with cows milk to resemble breast milk.

PARSLEY

Allergies	Coughs	Low Blood Pressure
Appetite	Digestion	Lumbago
Arthritis	Eyes	Menstruation
Asthma	Gall Bladder	**Pituitary**
Bad Breath	Gall Stones	Prostate
Bed Wetting	Gout	Spleen
Bites	Hay Fever	Thyroid
Bruises	Kidneys	Water Retention
Cancer	Liver	

Parsley will dry up mother's milk after birth.

PASSION FLOWER

Alcoholism	High Blood Pressure	Sleep
Fever	Insomnia	
Headaches	**Nerves**	

PEACH

Bladder	Morning Sickness	**Water Retention**
Congestion	Nerves	Wounds
Insomnia	Sleep	
Laxative	Vomiting	

PENNYROYAL

Colds	Gout	Nausea
Colic	Headache	Nerves
Congestion	Itching	Perspiration
Convulsions	Lungs	Rashes
Cramps	Menstruation	Skin Disease
Fever	Mucous	Sun Stroke

Toothache   Ulcers

Should not be taken during early pregnancy as it may cause abortion.

PEPPERMINT

Appetite   Diverticulitis   Menstruation
Boils   Dizziness   Migraine Headaches
Bronchitis   Flu   Morning Sickness
Chills   Gall Bladder   Muscle Spasms
Cholera   **Gas**   Nausea
Colds   Headache   Nerves
Colic   **Heartburn**   Nightmares
Colitis   Insanity   Shingles
Cough   Insomnia   Smoking
Cramps (stomach) Itching   Stimulant
Diarrhea   Liver
Digestion   Measles

Use as a bath for Itching Skin.

PLANTAIN

Bites   Hemorrhoids   Poisoning
Bladder   Hoarseness   Stomach
Bleeding   Itching   Thrush
Burns   Kidneys   Tumors
Diarrhea   Leucorrhea   Ulcers
Eyes   Lumbago   Vagina
Frigidity   Lungs   **Wounds**
Hemorrhage   Menstruation

PLEURISY ROOT

Asthma   Flu   Pneumonia
Bronchitis   **Lungs**   Rheumatic Fever
Chicken Pox   Measles   Scarlet Fever
Circulation   Menstruation   Typhus
Contagious Diseases Mucous   Water Retention
Coughs   Perspiration
Fever   Pleurisy

Pleurisy Root is used to relax the capillaries.

POKE WEED

Arthritis	Hemorrhoids	Pain
Breasts	Infection	Parasites
Cancer	**Inflammation**	Rheumatism
Glands	Laxative	Skin Disease
Goiter	Liver	Thyroid
Gums	Lumbago	Tremors

PSYLLIUM

Colon	**Constipation**	Hemorrhoids
Colitis	**Diverticulitis**	Ulcers

Psyllium helps to lubricate and heal the intestinal tract. It also moistens and acts as a bulk agent.

QUEEN OF THE MEADOW

Diabetes	Nerves	Uterus
Gravel	Prostate	Vagina
Kidneys	Rheumatism	Water Retention
Lumbago	Urination	

RASPBERRY

Afterpain	Dysentery	Mucous Membranes
Birth Defects	Eyewash	Nausea
Bronchitis	Female Organs	Nerves
Canker	**Flu**	**Pregnancy**
Childbirth	Lactation	Rheumatism
Colds	Leucorrhea	Stomach
Constipation	Measles	Throat
Coughs	Menstruation	Ulcers
Diabetes	**Morning Sickness**	Uterus
Diarrhea	Mouth Sores	

RED CLOVER

Blood Purifier	**Nerves**	Scarlet Fever
Boils	Psoriasis	Skin Diseases
Cancer	Rheumatism	

REDMOND CLAY

Acne   **Bee Stings**

Should be used externally for skin problems as a pack.

ROSE HIPS

Arteriosclerosis	Circulation	Fever
Bee Stings	Colds	Heart
Bites	Contagious Diseases	Jaundice
Bruises	Emphysema	Kidneys

Very high in Vitamin C.

ROSEMARY

Appetite	Blood Pressure	Prostate
Baldness	Migraine Headaches	

RUE

Arteriosclerosis	Gout	Menstruation
Blood Pressure	Hypoglycemia	Nerves
Colic	Hysteria	Rheumatism
Cough	Insanity	Sciatica
Dizziness	Joints	Stomach
Eyes	Measles	Thrush

Do not use during Pregnancy. Rue repels flies and other insects. When a woman is going through menopause, Rue helps nervous Heart Palpitations. It should be taken between meals.

SAFFRON – SAFFLOWERS

Appetite	Frigidity	Measles
Arthritis	**Gas**	Menstruation
Bronchitis	**Gout**	Psoriasis
Digestion	Heart	**Uric Acid**
Diuretic	**Heartburn**	**Water Retention**

Saffron is used by Hypoglycemics to alleviate Fatigue and Muscle Cramps after exertion or exercise.

SAGE

Baldness	Hair	Nerves
Bites	Headache	Night Sweats
Bronchitis	Hoarseness	Palsy
Dandruff	Lactation	Parasites
Diarrhea	Laryngitis	Sex Desire
Digestion	Lungs	Skin Disease
Dizziness	Menstruation	Stomach
Fever	Morning Sickness	Throat
Flu	Mouth	Tonsillitis
Gas	**Nausea**	Ulcers

Sage tea can be used to rinse the hair to maintain color.

SARSAPARILLA

Acne	Eyes	Mucous
Age Spots	Fevers	Psoriasis
Blood Purifier	Gout	Ringworm
Boils	Heartburn	Rheumatism
Colds	**Hot Flashes**	

Sarsaparilla contains **hormones** for both systems. When it is used with Ginseng, it helps teen-age boys with complexion problems due to hormone imbalance.

SAW PALMETTO

Alcoholism	Bronchitis	Glands
Asthma	Colds	Prostate
Bladder	Diabetes	
Breasts	Frigidity	

Saw Palmetto helps underweight people to **gain weight.** It also has been used to help develop small breasts.

SCULLCAP

Alcoholism	Hypoglycemia	**Nerves**
Blood Pressure	Indigestion	Paralysis
Convulsions	Insanity	**Rabies**
Epilepsy	Insect Bites	Rheumatism
Hangovers	**Insomnia**	Sex Desire
Hysteria	Mumps	Smoking

SENNA

Jaundice   Laxative   Liver

Because Senna can cause griping, it should be used in combination with other herbs. Soak raisins in Senna tea for Parasites.

SHEPHERD'S PURSE

Arteriosclerosis	Heart	Menstruation
Blood Pressure	Hemorrhage	Migraine Headache
Bowels	Hemorrhoids	Uterus
Diuretic	Kidneys	Vagina
Dizziness	Measles	
Fever	Menopause	

Shepherd's Purse constricts blood vessels and thereby raises the Blood Pressure. It normalizes either high or low Blood Pressure however. Because it contracts the intestines, it is helpful in difficult Bowel movements. Shepherd's Purse helps stop bleeding from Lungs and Bronchial Tubes.

SLIPPERY ELM

Asthma	**Diaper Rash**	Leucorrhea
Bladder	**Diarrhea**	Lungs
Boils	**Digestion**	Ovaries
Bowels	Diuretic	Sex Stimulant
Bronchitis	**Diverticulitis**	Smoking
Burns	**Dysentery**	Stomach
Cancer	Eczema	Tonsillitis
Colon	Eyes	Ulcers
Colitis	Flu	Urination
Constipation	Gas	Uterus
Cramps	Hemorrhage	Vagina
Cough	Hoarseness	Wounds
Cystitis	Inflammation	

Slippery Elm can be used internally, as a poultice, or in an enema. It can be used as a bolus for uterine problems.

SPEARMINT (See PEPPERMINT)

SQUAW VINE

Childbirth	Gravel	Nerves
Eyewash	**Menstruation**	Urination

ST. JOHNSWORT

Afterpain	Gout	Lungs
Anemia	Heart	Menstruation
Bed Wetting	Hemorrhage	Nerves
Coughs	Hysteria	Urination
Diarrhea	Jaundice	Wounds

STRAWBERRY (See RASPBERRY)

THYME

Asthma	Headache	Mucous Membranes
Cramps	**Heartburn**	Nerves
Diarrhea	Lungs	Nightmares
Digestion	Menstruation	Shingles
Fever	**Migraine Headache**	Stomach
Flu	Mucous	Whooping Cough

TURKEY RHUBARB

Colon	Constipation	Croup

UVA URSI

Bed Wetting	Hemorrhoids	Pancreas
Bladder	Kidneys	Piles
Bronchitis	Leucorrhea	Prostate
Cystitis	Liver	Spleen
Diabetes	Lumbago	Uterus
Digestion	Menstruation	Vagina
Dysentery	Mucous Membranes	Venereal Disease
Female Problems	Obesity	

VALERIAN ROOT

Acne	Colds	Convulsions
Afterpain	Colic	Digestion
Blood Pressure	Contagious Disease	Fever

Gas	Measles	Parasites
Hangovers	Menstruation	Scarlet Fever
Heart	Migraine Headaches	Shock
Heartburn	Nerves	Smoking
Hypoglycemia	Pain	Spasms
Hysteria	Palsy	Stomach
Insomnia	Paralysis	Ulcers

VERVAIN

Convulsions	Measles	Spleen
Cough	Menstruation	Wounds
Gall Stones	Nerves	
Headache	Smoking	

WHITE OAK BARK

Acne	Jaundice	Skin Disease
Bladder	Kidneys	**Teeth**
Bruises	**Leucorrhea**	**Thrush**
Fever	Liver	Tonsillitis
Fever Blisters	Menstruation	Toothache
Gall Bladder	**Mouth**	**Ulcers**
Goiter	Nose	Urination
Gums	Parasites	Uterus
Hemorrhage	Pyorrhea	Vagina
Hemorrhoids	Ringworm	**Varicose Veins**

White Oak Bark Tea will set loose teeth and also heal most sores in mouth. A cloth wrung out of White Oak Bark Tea and applied directly to Varicose Veins helps reduce the size. The herb is used internally also.

WILD YAM

| Menstruation | Nausea | Stomach |
| Morning Sickness | Pain | Ulcers |

Wild Yam is especially good for the Stomach as it relieves gas pains.

WILLOW

Arthritis	Burns	Dandruff
Baldness	Bursitis	Eyes
Bed Wetting	Convulsions	Fever

Gall Stones
Gas
Gout

Gums
Headache
Hemorrhage

Rheumatism
Sex Depressant
Wounds

WINTERGREEN

Diabetes
Eyes

Fever
Headache

Venereal Disease

WITCH HAZEL

Eyes
Gums
Hemorrhage

Mucous Membranes
Sinus
Varicose Veins

Venereal Disease
Wounds

WOOD BETONY

Asthma
Bed Wetting
Bladder
Bronchitis
Convulsions
Cough
Cramps
Diarrhea
Dizziness
Gout

Headache
Heart
Heartburn
Indigestion
Inflammation
Insanity
Kidneys
Migraine Headache
Menstruation
Nerves

Pain
Palsy
Parasites
Perspiration
Sprains
Tonsillitis
Varicose Veins
Wounds

Wood Betony is good to heal old sores.

WORMWOOD

Appetite
Arthritis
Boils
Bursitis
Childbirth

Circulation
Diarrhea
Fever
Gall Bladder
Gas

Heartburn
Indigestion
Liver
Parasites
Stomach

YARROW

Appetite
Arthritis
Baldness
Bladder

Bleeding
Blood Purifier
Bursitis
Colds

Colon
Congestion
Contagious Disease
Diabetes

Ear Infection	Liver	Perspiration
Fever	Lungs	Pleurisy
Flu	Measles	Skin
Hemorrhage (Lungs)	Menstruation	Spleen
Hemorrhoids	Mucous Membranes	Urination
Jaundice	Night Sweats	Uterus
Kidney	Piles	

Yarrow is good for Mucous discharge from the bladder. As a shampoo, use the tea for baldness.

YELLOW DOCK

Acne	Ear (running)	Poison Ivy
Anemia	Endurance	Poison Oak
Bladder	Energy	Psoriasis
Bleeding	Eyes	Scarlet Fever
Blood Purifier	Fatigue	Spleen
Boils	Gall Bladder	Swelling
Cancer	Itching	Tumors
Chicken Pox	**Liver**	Venereal Disease
Earache	Paralysis	Vitality
Ear Infection	Pituitary	

Yellow Dock is helpful for ulcerated Eyelids.

YERBA SANTA

Asthma	Fever	Mucous
Bladder	Headache	Rheumatism
Blood Purifier	Hemorrhage	Sprains
Bronchitis	Insect Bites	Tuberculosis
Bruises	Laryngitis	Wounds
Colds	Lungs	
Coughs	Mouthwash	

Chapter 3

HERBAL COMBINATIONS

For convenience and space, the following groups of herbs herea-after will be referred to by the number on the left.

The author does not directly or indirectly dispense medical advice or prescribe the use of herbs as a form of treatment for sickness without medical approval.

(1) . . . . .Cayenne, Valerian Root, Wild Lettuce.

Afterpain	Headache	Toothache
Arthritis	Pain	
Cramps	Rheumatism	

(2) . . . . .Alfalfa, Black Cohosh, Bromalain Powder, Burdock Root, Cayenne, Centaury, Chaparral, Comfrey, Lobelia, Poke Weed, Yarrow, Yucca.

Arthritis	Gout	Rheumatism
Bursitis	Lupus	

(3) . . . . .Barberry, Burdock, Cascara Sagrada, Chaparral, Dandelion, Licorice, Red Clover, Sarsaparilla, Yarrow, Yellow Dock.

Acne	Convulsions	Pancreas
Age Spots	Dandruff	Psoriasis
Anemia	Eczema	Ringworm
Bee Stings	Gangrene	Skin Disease
Blood Poisoning	Infection	Smoking
Blood Purifier	Inflammation	Spleen
Boils	Itching	Tumors
Cancer	Jaundice	Venereal Disease
Canker	Liver	Wounds
Cleansing	Lupus	
Contagious Diseases	Lymph	

(4). . . . . .Alfalfa, Comfrey, Horsetail, Irish Moss, Lobelia

Afterpain	Gout	Obesity
Allergies	Hair	Pain
Arteriosclerosis	Headaches	Pleurisy
Arthritis	Hypoglycemia	Pregnancy
Bursitis	Hysteria	Psoriasis
Baldness	Insomnia	Rheumatism
Bee Stings	Jaundice	Sciatica
Bites	Joints	Seizures
Childbirth	Lactation	Stomach
Colds	Liver	Teeth
Colitis	Lumbago	Toothache
Cramps	Lupus	Ulcers
Eczema	Migraine Headaches	Varicose Veins
Fingernails	Multiple Sclerosis	Water Retention
Flu	Nerves	Wounds
Fractures	Nightmares	

(5). . . . . .Cayenne, Camomile, Golden Seal, Lemon Grass, Myrrh, Peppermint, Rose Hips, Sage, Yarrow.

Colds	Flu	Mucous
Ear Infection		

(6). . . . . .Black Cohosh, Cayenne, Ginger, Hops, Mistletoe, St. Johnswort, Valerian, Wood Betony.

Arthritis	Insanity	Sciatica
Convulsions	Menopause	Shingles
Eczema	Nerves	St. Vitus Dance
Hyperactivity	Nightmares	

(7). . . . . .Bayberry, Eyebright, Golden Seal.

Eyes	Diabetes	Hayfever

Can take internally or use as a wash.

(8). . . . . .Blessed Thistle, Cayenne, Ginger, Golden Seal, Gravel Root, Lobelia, Marshmallow Root, Parsley, Raspberry Leaves.

Acne	Hot Flashes	Sterility
Breasts	Menopause	Uterus
Female Problems	Menstrual Cramps	Vagina
Hormone Balance	Morning Sickness	

After a hysterectomy it helps to balance hormones. This combination helps all menstrual difficulties: Excessive Menstruation, Suppressed Menstruation, or Difficult Menstruation.

(9). . . . . .Alfalfa, Bayberry, Cayenne, Comfrey, Echinacea, Ginger, Ginseng, Lobelia, Myrrh.

Colds	Gas	Wounds
Digestion	Glands	Muscular Aches
Flu	Sore Throat	& Pains

(10). . . . . .Black Cohosh, Blessed Thistle, Pleurisy Root, Scullcap.

Allergies	Bronchitis	Mucous
Asthma	Hayfever	Sinuses

(11). . . . . .Cayenne, Ginger, Golden Seal, Licorice.

Flu	Nausea	Vomiting
Morning Sickness	Stomach	

(12). . . . . .Cayenne, Ginseng, Gotu Kola.

Age Spots	Insanity	Sterility
Drug Withdrawal	Longevity	Tetanus
Endurance	Memory	Vitality
Energy	Pituitary	
Fatigue	Senility	

This combination used with Camomile and Licorice has been excellent for Drug Withdrawal.

(13). . . . . .Cayenne, Hawthorn.

Adrenal Glands	Endurance	Heart
Arteriosclerosis	Energy	Shock
Blood Pressure	Fatigue	Vitality

See directions at beginning of chapter.

(14). . . . . .Hops, Scullcap, Valerian Root.

Convulsions	Insomnia	Palsy
Hysteria	Nerves	Paralysis
Indigestion	Nightmares	Sex Depressant
Insanity	Pain	St. Vitus Dance

(15). . . . . .Dandelion, Licorice, Horseradish, Safflowers.

| Adrenal Glands | Anemia | Hypoglycemia |

(16). . . . . .Cayenne, Echinacea, Myrrh, Poke Root.

Breast Infection	Flu	Mucous
Contagious Diseases	Gangrene	Rheumatic Fever
Ear Infection	Infection	Throat
Fever	Lymph Glands	Tonsillitis

This combination is used the same as (17). It has Myrrh in place of Golden Seal for people with Hypoglycemia who are unable to use Golden Seal.

(17). . . . . .Cayenne, Echinacea, Golden Seal, Poke Root.

Breast Infection	Flu	Mucous
Contagious Diseases	Gangrene	Rheumatic Fever
Ear Infection	Infection	Throat
Fever	Lymph Glands	Tonsillitis

(18). . . . . .Camomile, Dandelion, Juniper, Parsley, Uva-Ursi.

| Bed Wetting | Diuretic | Kidneys |
| Bladder | | |

(19). . . . . .Alfalfa, Dandelion, Kelp.

Anemia	Energy	Parkinson's Disease
Birth Defects	Fatigue	Pituitary Gland
Convulsions	Hair	Senility
Cramps	Kidneys	Water Retention
Endurance	Multiple Sclerosis	

Also for fleas in animals.

(20)............Barberry, Cascara Sagrada, Cayenne, Ginger,
Lobelia, Red Clover.

Bad Breath	Constipation	Fever
Cleansing	Croup	Parasites
Colitis	Diverticulitis	Sinuses
Colon	Dysentery	

This combination of herbs helps to break up impactions in the colon,
also parasites, and is very healing. One doctor has fantastic success
giving his patients 6 to 12 a day. It is best to start slow and build up
to your body's requirements.

(21)............Comfrey, Lobelia, Marshmallow, Mullein,
Slippery Elm.

Allergies	Emphysema	Mucous
Asthma	Hayfever	Pneumonia
Bronchitis	Hoarseness	Sinuses
Cough	Lungs	Smoking

(22)............ Angelica, Birch Leaves, Blessed Thistle,
Camomile, Dandelion, Gentian, Golden Rod,
Horsetail, Liverworth Leaves, Lobelia, Parsley,
Red Beet.

Acne	Gall Bladder	Pancreas
Age Spots	Gall Stones	Rheumatic Fever
Cleansing	Jaundice	Spleen
Dizziness	Liver	

(23)............Bistort, Blueberry Leaves, Buchu, Comfrey,
Dandelion, Eyebright, Garlic, Golden Seal,
Juniper, Marshmallow, Uva Ursi, Yarrow.

Bladder	Infection	Pancreas
Diabetes	Kidneys	

(24)............Comfrey, Golden Seal, Slippery Elm.

Boils	Flu	Lumbago
Breaks	Fractures	Poultice
Burns	Gangrene	Rheumatism
Cuts	Infection	Wounds

One doctor is getting good results with his patients who suffer from back problems. It is known as the "bone knitter."

(25). . . . . .Cayenne, Red Clover, Soy.

Hypoglycemia   Protein Supplement

(26). . . . . .Black Cohosh, Cayenne, Ginger, Golden Seal, Gotu Kola, Kelp, Licorice, Lobelia.

Bladder   Hormone Balance   Prostate
Kidneys

Zinc is very important in Prostate Problems.

(27). . . . . .Black Walnut, Chickweed, Dandelion, Echinacea, Fennel, Gotu Kola, Hawthorn, Licorice, Mandrake, Papaya, Saffron.

Cleanser   Glands   Obesity
Constipation

Add more Chickweed for more rapid weight loss.

(28). . . . . .Barberry, Black Walnut, Bugle Weed, Catnip, Chickweed, Comfrey, Cyani Flowers, Dandelion, Echinacea, Fenugreek, Gentian, Golden Seal, Irish Moss, Mandrake, Myrrh Gum, Pink Root, Poke Root, Safflowers, St. Johnswort, Yellow Dock.

Cancer   Constipation   Tumors
Cleanser   Multiple Sclerosis
Colon   Parasites

This combination works better for Parasites when taken with extra Black Walnut. As this combination breaks toxins from the body, it is suggested that enemas be used. (See chapter on Cleansing.)

(29). . . . . .Cayenne, Irish Moss, Kelp, Parsley.

Epilepsy   Goiter   Sore Throat
Fatigue   Pituitary   Thyroid

This combination helps the Thyroid Gland produce the thyroxine which regulates either underactive or overactive Thyroid. Most people who suffer from Epilepsy seem to have an underactive Thyroid.

(30). . . . . .Cayenne, Golden Seal, Myrrh.

Canker	Dysentary	Pyorrhea
Colitis	Fever Blisters	Stomach
Colon	Gums	Thrush
Cuts	Heartburn	Ulcers
Diverticulitis	Indigestion	

(31). . . . . .Alfalfa, Cayenne, Comfrey, Kelp, Lemon Grass, Rose Hips, Soy Beans, Yeast.

Balanced vitamin and mineral combination. Since it would be good for most health problems we will not list it under each problem.

(32). . . . . .Cayenne, Chickweed, Damiana, Echinacea, Garlic, Ginseng, Gotu Kola, Periwinkle, Sarsaparilla, Saw Palmetto.

Frigidity	Menopause	Sterility
Hormone Imbalance	Parkinson's Disease	
Hot Flashes	Sex Stimulant	

This helps to rebuild and strengthen the sex glands.

(33). . . . . .Black Cohosh, Lobelia, Pennyroyal, Raspberry , Squaw Vine.

Childbirth

Strengthens Uterus thereby making Childbirth easier and often eliminates stitches.

See directions at beginning of chapter.

Chapter 4

HEALTH PROBLEMS

The author does not directly or indirectly dispense medical advice or prescribe the use of herbs as a form of treatment for sickness without medical approval. Nutritionists and other experts in the field of health and nutrition hold widely varying views. It is not the intent of the author to diagnose or prescribe. Our intent is only to offer health information to help you cooperate with your doctor in your mutual problem of building health. In the event you use this information without your doctor's approval, you are prescribing for yourself, which is your constitutional right, but the publisher assumes no responsibility.

The herbs are used in capsules or teas unless otherwise indicated. The words in bold type are the ones with which we have had the most experience. See Chapter 3 for an explanation of number references.

ACNE

(3)	Chickweed	Sarsaparilla
(8)	Dandelion	Valerian Root
(22)	Echinacea	**White Oak Bark**
Burdock	Ginseng	**Yellow Dock**
Cayenne	Jojoba	
Chaparral	Redmond Clay	

Any of these herbs can be used internally, or as an external scrub.
(3) helps to purify and cleanse the blood.
(8) helps to balance the female hormones.
Ginseng and Sarsaparilla help to balance the male hormones.
Vitamins: A, B, C, E

AFTERPAIN (See also CHILDBIRTH)

(1)	Raspberry	Valerian Root
(4)	**St. Johnswort**	Wormwood

AGE SPOTS

(3)	Dandelion	Licorice
(12)	Ginseng	Sarsaparilla
(22)	Gotu Kola	

Age spots seem to disappear when the liver and blood are cleansed.
Vitamins: B, E

ALCOHOLISM

Cayenne	Passion Flower	Scullcap
Golden Seal	Saw Palmetto	Valerian Root

These herbs help to cleanse the system and take away the taste for
alcohol.
Vitamins: A, B, C, E
Minerals: Magnesium

ALLERGIES

(4)	Chickweed	Marshmallow
(10)	Comfrey	Papaya
(21)	Eyebright	Parsley
Alfalfa	Fenugreek	
Bee Pollen	Golden Seal	
Burdock	Juniper Berries	
Chaparral	Lobelia	

Vitamins: A, C, E, Pantothenic Acid
Minerals: Calcium

ANEMIA

(3)	Comfrey	St. Johnswort
(19)	**Dandelion**	**Yellow Dock**
Alfalfa	Fenugreek	
Barberry	Kelp	

(3) cleanses and purifies the blood, Yellow Dock is very high in natural iron, and Dandelion contains the nutritive salts necessary to build good blood.
Vitamins: B, C, E, PABA

APPETITE

To Increase:

Alfalfa	Garlic	Oat Straw
Barberry	Gentian	Parsley
Blessed Thistle	Ginseng	Peppermint
Camomile	Golden Seal	Rosemary
Cayenne	Hops	Saffron (Safflowers)
Dandelion	Horseradish	Wormwood
Fennel	Juniper Berries	Yarrow

To Decrease:

Chickweed	Fennel

Fennel tends to normalize the appetite. If you don't have an appetite, it will increase it; on the other hand, if you have a large appetite, it helps decrease it.

ARTERIOSCLEROSIS

(4)	**Garlic**	Rue
(13)	Hawthorn	Shepherd's Purse
Cayenne	Rose Hips	

Vitamins: A, B, C, E
Minerals: Calcium, Magnesium

ARTHRITIS

(1)	**Burdock**	Oat Straw
(2)	Cayenne	Parsley
(4)	**Chaparral**	Poke Berries
(6)	**Comfrey**	Saffron
Alfalfa	Hawthorn	Willow
Black Cohosh	Juniper Berries	Wormwood
Blessed Thistle	**Licorice Root**	Yarrow
Brigham Tea	Lobelia	

Vitamins: B, C, E
Minerals: Calcium, Potassium

ASTHMA

(10)	Ginseng	Myrrh
(21)	Golden Seal	Parsley
Bee Pollen	Horseradish	Pleurisy Root
Black Cohosh	Hyssop	Saw Palmetto
Brigham Tea	Licorice Root	Slippery Elm
Camomile	**Lobelia**	Thyme
Cayenne	Marshmallow	Wood Betony
Chickweed	Mullein	Yerba Santa
Comfrey		

Honey has been used successfully. Tincture of Lobelia is used during an acute attack.
Vitamins: A, B, Pantothenic Acid

BAD BREATH

(20)	Echinacea	Myrrh
Alfalfa	Golden Seal	**Parsley**
Cloves	Irish Moss	

Bad Breath is usually a result of congestion in the colon. Green drinks are helpful. Cloves can be chewed for temporary clean breath. See recipe in back of book for Green Drink.
Vitamins: C

BALDNESS (Prevent Hair Loss)

(4)	**Jojoba Shampoo**	Watercress
Aloe Vera	Juniper	White Willow
Burdock	Nettle	Yarrow
Chaparral	Rosemary	(Shampoo with tea)
Horsetail	**Sage**	

Vitamins: B, C, E, Inosital

BED WETTING

(6)	Hops	St. Johnswort
(18)	Juniper	Willow
Bistort	Marshmallow	Wood Betony
Buchu	Oat Straw	Uva Ursi
Cornsilk	Parsley	
Fennel	Plantain	

47

One cup parsley tea 1 hour before bedtime will help.
Vitamins: A
Minerals: Magnesium

BEE STINGS (See also BITES)

(4)	Juniper	Redmond Clay
Black Cohosh	Parsley	Rose Hips
Hyssop	Plantain	Yerba Santa

Honey pulls stinger out and helps neutralize and counteract poison.
Apply ice until swelling and pain leaves an then apply the clay.
Vitamins: C
Minerals: Calcium, Magnesium

BIRTH DEFECTS (To Prevent)

(19)	**Kelp**	**Raspberry**

These herbs are all helpful in supplying proper nutrients during
pregnancy. Raspberry helps eliminate morning sickness and also
strengthens the uterus.
Vitamins: C, E
Minerals: Manganese, Phosphorus

BITES (All insects, including poisonous. See also BEE STINGS)

(4)	Fennel	Plantain
Bistort	Hyssop	Rose Hips
Black Cohosh	Juniper	Sage
Comfrey	Lobelia	Scullcap
Echinacea	Parsley	Yerba Santa

Vitamins: C
Minerals: Calcium, Magnesium

BLADDER (See also KIDNEYS, URINATION)

(18)	Comfrey	**Marshmallow**
(26)	Cornsilk	Oat Straw
Barberry	Echinacea	Peach
Blue Cohosh	Golden Seal	Plantain
Buchu	Horseradish	Saw Palmetto
Burdock	Hyssop	Slippery Elm
Camomile	Juniper	Uva Ursi

White Oak Bark	Yarrow	Yerba Santa
Wood Betony	Yellow Dock	

Marshmallow is used for bladder hemorrhage — 1 oz. in 1 pint of milk simmered slowly then take ½ cup each ½ hour.

BLEEDING (See HEMORRHAGE, WOUNDS)

BLOOD PRESSURE

High:

Barberry	**Garlic**	Scullcap
Black Cohosh	Hawthorn	Passion Flower
Blue Cohosh	Mistletoe	Valerian
Cayenne	Rue	

Low:

Brigham Tea	Hawthorn	Rosemary
Dandelion	Parsley	Shepherd's Purse

The following herbs are used to normalize both high and low blood pressure:

(13)	Garlic	Shepherd's Purse
Cayenne		

Vitamins: B, C, E
Minerals: Magnesium, Potassium

BLOOD PURIFIER

(3)	**Chaparral**	Sarsaparilla
Barberry	Comfrey	Spikenard
Black Cohosh	**Dandelion**	Yarrow
Blue Cohosh	Echinacea	**Yellow Dock**
Brigham Tea	Hyssop	Yerba Santa
Burdock	Licorice	
Camomile	Red Clover	

BOILS

(3)	Black Walnut	Chickweed
(24)	**Burdock**	Comfrey
Barberry	**Chaparral**	**Dandelion**

Echinacea	Nettle	Slippery Elm
Juniper	Oat Straw	Wormwood
Lobelia	Peppermint	**Yellow Dock**
Mullein	Red Clover	
Myrrh	Sarsaparilla	

Lobelia and Mullein are excellent as a poultice: 3 parts Mullein to 1 part Lobelia. The other herbs can be taken internally.

BREASTS

(8)	(17)	Saw Palmetto
(16)	Poke Root	

For lumps or caked breasts, Poke Root poultices help.
Vitamins: A, C, E

BRONCHITIS

(10)	Eucalyptus	Pleurisy Root
(21)	Fennel	Raspberry
Black Cohosh	Fenugreek	Sage
Camomile	Ginger	Saffron (Safflowers)
Catnip	Golden Seal	Saw Palmetto
Cayenne	Licorice	Slippery Elm
Chickweed	**Lobelia**	Uva Ursi
Comfrey	Mullein	Wood Betony
Dandelion	Peppermint	

Cayenne taken with Ginger cleans out bronchial tubes.
Vitamins: A, C, E

BRUISES (See also INFLAMMATION)

Comfrey	Lobelia	Rose Hips
Fenugreek	Mullein	White Oak Bark
Hyssop	Parsley	Yerba Santa

All of the above herbs are good taken internally and applied as a poultice.
Vitamins: C

The author does not directly or indirectly dispense medical advice or prescribe the use of herbs as a form of treatment for sickness without medical approval.

50

BURNS

(24)	Chickweed	Marshmallow
Aloe Vera	Comfrey	**Plantain**
Burdock	Golden Seal	Slippery Elm
Cayenne	Hyssop	Willow

Apply ice water and keep cloths wet and cold. For shock which accompanies extreme burns, take cayenne by mouth. Mix vitamin E with the (24), or apply the vitamin E directly on the burn and mix the (24) with mineral water. Aloe Vera is used both internally and as a poultice.
Vitamins: C, E

BURSITIS (See also ARTHRITIS, RHEUMATISM)

(2)	Comfrey	Willow
(4)	Kelp	Wormwood
Alfalfa	Lobelia	Yarrow
Burdock	Mullein	
Chaparral	Oat Straw	

Mullein is often used as a poultice to give relief externally.
Vitamins: C
Minerals: Calcium, Chlorine

CANCER (See also TUMORS. See also Cleansing Chapter)

(3)	Eucalyptus	Parsley
(28)	Garlic	Poke Root
Chaparral	Ginseng	Red Clover
Chickweed	Golden Seal	Slippery Elm
Dandelion Root	Irish Moss	Yellow Dock

Vitamins: A, B, C, E

CANKER (Mouth, Stomach, Colon)

(3)	Burdock	Myrrh
(30)	Chickweed	Raspberry
Bayberry	**Golden Seal**	

Vitamins: C, Niacin (B^3)

CATARACTS

(7)   Chaparral   Eyebright

(7) can be taken internally and also used as an eye wash by steeping 1 capsule in ¼ cup boiling water for 10 minutes then straining through a paper towel and washing the eyes morning and night. A drop of liquid honey dropped in the corner of the eye has helped in certain cases.
Vitamins: A, B

CHICKEN POX (See also CONTAGIOUS DISEASES)

Burdock	**Golden Seal**	Pleurisy Root
Ginger	**Lobelia**	**Yellow Dock**

Bathe the affected area in tea made from Burdock, Golden Seal and Yellow Dock. See *Herbalist Magazine, Volume 1 #1.*

CHILDBIRTH (See also AFTERPAIN, LACTATION PREGNANCY)

(4)	Kelp	Spikenard
(33)	Myrrh	Squaw Vine
Blue Cohosh	Shepherd's Purse	Raspberry

Myrrh can be applied to the navel after cord is removed to prevent infection.
Vitamins: C, E
Minerals: Calcium

CHILLS

Bayberry   **Cayenne**   Peppermint

Add a pinch of cayenne to Bayberry Tea.
Vitamins: E

CIRCULATION

Black Cohosh	Golden Seal	Pleurisy Root
Cayenne	Horseradish	Rose Hips
Chickweed	Hyssop	Wormwood

Cayenne increases the pulse rate while Black Cohosh slows the pulse rate.
Vitamins: C, E, Lecithin

CLEANSING (See Cleansing Chapter)

(3)	(28)	Dandelion
(20)	Burdock	Lobelia
(22)	Chickweed	Yellow Dock

Sometimes after heavy cleansing, the mucous lining in the bowel gets depleted and it is painful. Take ½ cup distilled water, add 1 Table-spoon cider vinegar, and 1 teaspoon honey with ¼ teaspoon cayenne and sip it several times a day. This helps to rebuild the mucous lining and heal the intestine.

COLDS (See also COUGH, FEVER, FLU, MUCOUS)

(4)	**Comfrey**	Raspberry
(5)	**Fenugreek**	Rose Hips
Bayberry	Garlic	Sarsaparilla
Brigham Tea	Ginger	Saw Palmetto
Camomile	Ginseng	Valerian
Catnip	Licorice	Yarrow
Cayenne	Peppermint	Yerba Santa

Vitamins: A, B, C, E
Minerals: Calcium

COLIC

Blue Cohosh	Pennyroyal	Valerian Root
Catnip	Peppermint	
Fennel	Rue	

COLITIS

(4)	Comfrey	Mandrake
(20)	Fenugreek	Myrrh
(30)	Ginger	Peppermint
Camomile	Golden Seal	Slippery Elm
Carob	Kelp	

Vitamins: B
Minerals: Calcium, Magnesium

COLON

(20)	Cascara Sagrada	Mullein
(28)	Chickweed	Myrrh
(30)	Comfrey	Psyllium
Bayberry	Fenugreek	Slippery Elm
Camomile	Hyssop	Turkey Rhubarb

Fenugreek helps to lubricate. Hyssop and Mullein is good for mucous in the Colon. ½ cup distilled water, 1 Tablespoon Cider Vinegar, 1 teaspoon honey and ¼ teaspoon cayenne will help heal the colon.

CONSTIPATION (See also COLITIS, COLON)

(20)	Dandelion	Psyllium
(28)	Ginger	Raspberry
Aloe Vera	Ginseng	Slippery Elm
Barberry	Golden Seal	Senna
Blessed Thistle	Licorice	Shepherd's Purse
Buckthorn	Mullein	Turkey Rhubarb
Cascara Sagrada	Mandrake	
Chickweed	Poke Root	

Aloe Vera is used internally and the leaf next to the stem is used — 1 oz. 4 to 5 times a day. Senna can cause griping so is usually used in combination with other herbs.

CONTAGIOUS DISEASES (See also CHICKEN POX, CROUP, FEVER, MEASLES, MUMPS, RHEUMATIC FEVER)

(3)	Garlic	Rose Hips
(16)	Ginger	Valerian Root
(17)	Lobelia	Yarrow
Catnip	Pleurisy Root	
Cayenne		

Garlic enemas are very helpful, also Ginger baths help.
(See *Herbalist Magazine* Volume 1 #1)

The numbers in parentheses refer to herbal combinations.
See pages 37-43.

CONVULSIONS

(3)	Cayenne	Pennyroyal
(4)	Fennel	Scullcap
(6)	Ginseng	Valerian
(14)	Hyssop	Vervain
(19)	Horsetail	Willow
(29)	Irish Moss	Wood Betony
Black Cohosh	**Lobelia**	
Blue Cohosh	Mistletoe	

Vitamins: A, B, C, D, E
Minerals: Calcium, Magnesium, Silicone, Zinc

COUGH

(21)	Horseradish	Pleurisy Root
Black Cohosh	Hyssop	Raspberry
Cascara Sagrada	Irish Moss	Rue
Cayenne	Juniper	Slippery Elm
Comfrey	**Licorice**	St. Johnswort
Fennel	**Lobelia**	Thyme
Fenugreek	Marshmallow	Vervain
Garlic	Mullein	Wood Betony
Ginger	Myrrh	Yerba Santa
Ginseng	Parsley	
Hops	Peppermint	

The following are used as tinctures (See chapter **Definitions and Directions)**

Anti Spasmodic	Lobelia	Yerba Santa

Vitamins: A, C

CRAMPS

Leg (Also Muscle Spasms):

(4)	Cayenne	Kelp
(19)	Chaparral	Peppermint
Alfalfa	Comfrey	Saffron (Safflowers)
Blue Cohosh	Dandelion	Thyme

Menstrual:

(1)	**(8)**	Ginger
(4)	Blue Cohosh	Pennyroyal

55

Stomach:

(11)	Cloves	**Peppermint**
Blessed Thistle	Fennel	Slippery Elm
Camomile	Garlic	Thyme
Cayenne	Ginger	

The single herbs used as a tea seem to give best results.
Vitamins: B, E, D
Minerals: Calcium, Magnesium

CROUP (See also CONTAGIOUS DISEASES)

(20)	Eucalyptus	Lobelia
Cascara Sagrada	Garlic	Mullein
Catnip	Ginger	Turkey Rhubarb

Tincture of Lobelia is good for an acute attack. Ginger as a bath is good. The Eucalyptus Oil through a steamer helps. Catnip enemas are very beneficial.
(See *Herbalist Magazine,* Volume 1 #1)

CUTS (See WOUNDS)

CYSTITIS (See BLADDER)

DANDRUFF (See also SKIN DISEASES)

(3)	**Jojoba Shampoo**	Willow
Camomile	Nettle	Yarrow
Chaparral	**Sage**	

Chaparral and Yarrow can both be used as a tea on the head as well as taken internally.
Vitamins: B

DIABETES

(7)	Comfrey Root	Kelp
(23)	Dandelion	Marshmallow
Alfalfa	Eyebright	Queen of the Meadow
Blue Berries	False Unicorn	Raspberry
Blue Cohosh	Fenugreek	Saw Palmetto
Buchu	**Golden Seal**	Uva Ursi
Cayenne	Horsetail	Wintergreen
Chickweed	Juniper	Yarrow

Buchu is good in the first stages of Diabetes. (7) and Eyebright are used as an eyewash as well as internally.
Vitamins: A, B, C, E
Minerals: Potassium

DIAPER RASH (See also SKIN DISEASE)

Mullein   Slippery Elm

Blend the leaf of Mullein with Vitamin E and apply locally. Slippery Elm is used internally and also applied in a paste topically.

DIARRHEA

Barberry	Comfrey	Plantain
Bayberry	Garlic	**Raspberry**
Bistort	Ginger	Sage
Black Cohosh	Hyssop	**Slippery Elm**
Black Walnut	Mullein	St. Johnswort
Carob	Nutmeg	Thyme
Catnip	Peppermint	Wood Betony
Cloves	Periwinkle	

Take ½ teaspoon Nutmeg several times a day. Raspberry and Slippery Elm are used in an enema as well as internally. For Slippery Elm, use 1 Tablespoon powdered Slippery Elm to 1 bag of water. Raspberry is used as a tea.
Vitamins: B, C, Niacin
Minerals: Magnesium

DIGESTION (See also INDIGESTION)

(30)	Fenugreek	**Saffron (Safflowers)**
Alfalfa	Ginger	Sage
Barberry	Ginseng	Slippery Elm
Bayberry	Golden Seal	Thyme
Blessed Thistle	Horseradish	Uva Ursi
Carob	Hyssop	Valerian Root
Cascara Sagrada	Lobelia	Wood Betony
Cayenne	**Papaya**	Wormwood
Comfrey	Parsley	
Fennel	**Peppermint**	

Vitamins: B

DIURETIC (See WATER RETENTION)

DIVERTICULITIS (See also COLON. See also Cleansing Chapter)

(20)	Garlic	**Psyllium**
(30)	Papaya	**Slippery Elm**
Camomile	Peppermint	

DIZZINESS (See also Cleansing Chapter)

(22)	**Peppermint**	Shepherd's Purse
Camomile	Rue	Wood Betony
Catnip	Sage	

DOUCHE (See also **VAGINA**)

Barberry	**Garlic**	Plantain
Bistort	Ginger	Slippery Elm
Black Walnut	**Golden Seal**	White Oak Bark
Blue Cohosh	Magnolia	Witch Hazel
Cayenne	Marshmallow	
Fenugreek	Myrrh	

Bistort is used for bleeding from the vagina. Marshmallow tea is used for any vaginal irritation. Fresh Garlic is for any problem in uterus or vagina — put 4 or 5 cloves in blender with 1 quart water and blend. Cayenne and Garlic makes an excellent douche together.

DRUG WITHDRAWAL

| (12) | **Camomile** | **Licorice Root** |

These herbs taken together have helped those who have wanted to get off drugs.
Vitamins: B, C, E

DYSENTERY (See also COLON, DIARRHEA)

| (20) | Bayberry | **Slippery Elm** |
| (30) | **Raspberry** | Uva Ursi |

EAR INFECTION

| (5) | (16) | (17) |

| Aloe Vera | **Lobelia** | Yarrow |
| Hops | **Mullein** | Yellow Dock |

B and B Tincture, and Oil of Mullein are good to use as drops in ear. (See Chapter on **Definitions and Directions.**) Yellow Dock Tea is good for running ears. Baked onion is placed on ear for relief. Tincture of Lobelia used as drops helps relieve pain.
Vitamins: A, C, E

ECZEMA (See also SKIN DISEASE)

(3)	**(20)**	Comfrey
(4)	Aloe Vera	Kelp
(6)	Burdock	Slippery Elm

Aloe Vera can be used both internally and externally.
Vitamins: A, B, C, Lecithin, PABA
Minerals: Calcium

EMPHYSEMA (See also LUNGS, SMOKING)

(21)	**Fenugreek**	Rose Hips
Comfrey	Garlic	
Fennel	Licorice	

Comfrey and Fenugreek are good used together.
Vitamins: A, B, C, E

ENDURANCE & ENERGY (See also FATIGUE)

(12)	Dandelion	Hawthorn
(13)	Fennel	**Licorice Root**
(19)	Ginger	Yellow Dock
Burdock	**Ginseng**	
Cayenne	Gotu Kola	

Vitamins: E

EPILEPSY (See CONVULSIONS)

EYES

| **(7)** | Camomile | Chaparral |
| Bayberry | Cayenne | **Eyebright** |

Fennel	Oat Straw	Squaw Vine
Fenugreek	Parsley	Willow
Golden Seal	Plantain	Witch Hazel
Horsetail	**Raspberry**	Wintergreen
Hyssop	Rue	Yellow Dock
Marshmallow	Sarsaparilla	
Mullein	Slippery Elm	

(7) is used by steeping 1 capsule in ¼ cup boiling water and straining through paper towel, then used to drop in the eye. Hyssop packs help black eyes.
Vitamins: A

FATIGUE (See also ENDURANCE, ENERGY)

(12)	**Cayenne**	Saffron (Safflowers)
(13)	Comfrey	**Yellow Dock**
(19)	**Dandelion**	
(29)	Gotu Kola	

Gotu Kola is especially good for Mental Fatigue. Saffron is used for those who suffer from Hypoglycemia in that it relieves muscle aches and cramps when exercising.
Vitamins: E, Niacin

FEET

Camomile	Horsetail

Camomile is good for Callouses and Corns. Horsetail Tea helps foot odors and foot perspiration.

FEMALE PROBLEMS (See BREASTS, FRIGIDITY, HEMORRHAGE, LACTATION, MENOPAUSE, MENSTRUATION, MISCARRIAGE, MORNING SICKNESS, PREGNANCY, STERILITY, UTERUS)

FEVER

(16)	Echinacea	Magnolia
(17)	Eucalyptus	Mandrake
(20)	Fenugreek	Passion Flower
Blessed Thistle	Garlic	Pennyroyal
Brigham Tea	Ginseng	Pleurisy Root
Catnip	Hops	Rose Hips
Dandelion	Lobelia	Sage

60

Sarsaparilla	White Oak Bark	Yarrow
Shepherd's Purse	Willow	Yerba Santa
Thyme	Wintergreen	
Valerian	Wormwood	

Catnip Tea Enema is one of the best things one can do for a fever as it helps clear congested areas from the colon. Fever is usually caused by a blockage in the body.
Vitamins: C

FEVER BLISTERS

| (30) | Aloe Vera | White Oak Bark |

Vitamins: C

FINGERNAILS

(4)   **Horsetail**

Horsetail helps strengthen fingernails because of the high silica content. Silica is necessary for calcium absorption.
Vitamins: B
Minerals: Calcium

FLU

(5)	Ginger	Sage
(4)	Golden Seal	Slippery Elm
(9)	Marshmallow	Thyme
(11)	Peppermint	Yarrow
(16)	Pleurisy Root	
(17)	Raspberry	

(11) is good for intestinal flu and vomiting.
Vitamins: A, C, E
Minerals: Calcium

FRACTURES

| (4) | (24) | Comfrey |

The above herbs help to knit the bones, and also are very high in calcium.
Minerals: Calcium, Magnesium

FRIGIDITY (See also STERILITY)

(32)	Fenugreek	Saffron (Safflowers)
Chickweed	Ginseng	Sarsaparilla
Damiana	Plantain	Saw Palmetto

Mix Damiana and Saw Palmetto in equal parts.
Vitamins: E

FROST BITE

Oat Straw

Use as a wash externally.

GALL BLADDER (See also GALL STONES)

(22)	Dandelion	Oat Straw
Barberry	Fennel	Parsley
Blessed Thistle	Garlic	Peppermint
Buckthorn	Golden Seal	White Oak Bark
Burdock	Horsetail	Wormwood
Cascara Sagrada	Hyssop	Yellow Dock
Comfrey	Mistletoe	

Vitamins: A, B, C, D, E

GALL STONES (See also GALL BLADDER)

(22)	**Cascara Sagrada**	Parsley
Barberry	Dandelion	Vervain
Buckthorn	Hyssop	Willow
Burdock	Mandrake	

Three Day Gall Stone Cleanse: Apple Juice every day and each night take ½ cup olive oil and ½ cup lemon juice and go to bed. Take enema every morning. Alternate cleanse: 2 days of nothing but apple juice, and on third morning, ½ cup olive oil and ½ cup lemon juice and a garlic enema.

GANGRENE (See also INFECTION)

(3)	(17)	Camomile
(16)	(24)	

Camomile poultice to prevent gangrene.
Vitamins: C, E

62

GAS (See also COLON, STOMACH)

Colon:

Barberry	**Ginger**	Ginseng
Catnip		

Stomach:

Barberry	Gentian	Slippery Elm
Camomile	Hyssop	Spearmint
Catnip	Juniper	Valerian
Cayenne	Papaya	Willow
Fennel	**Peppermint**	Wormwood
Garlic	Saffron (Safflowers)	
Ginger	**Sage**	

Vitamins: B

GOITER (see also THYROID)

(29)	Poke Root	White Oak Bark
Kelp		

GONORRHEA (See VENERAL DISEASE)

GRAVEL & STONES (GALL BLADDER, KIDNEYS)

Catnip	Oat Straw	Parsley

GOUT (See also ARTHRITIS, RHEUMATISM)

(2)	Fennel	**Saffron (Safflowers)**
(4)	Gentian	Sarsaparilla
Alfalfa	Horseradish	St. Johnswort
Buckthorn	Oat Straw	Willow
Burdock	Parsley	Wood Betony
Comfrey	Pennyroyal	

Vitamins: B, C, E
Minerals: Potassium

GUMS

(30)	Echinacea	**White Oak Bark**
Barberry	Golden Seal	Willow
Bistort	Myrrh	Witch Hazel
Comfrey	Poke Root	

Vitamins: C

HAIR (See also BALDNESS, DANDRUFF)

(4)   Aloe Vera   **Jojoba Shampoo**
(19)

(4) helps split ends. Rub Aloe Vera on scalp. PABA to retain color.
Vitamins: B, PABA

HALITOSIS (See BAD BREATH)

HANGOVER (See ALCOHOLISM)

HAYFEVER

(7)	**Cayenne**	Golden Seal
(10)	Chaparral	Juniper
(21)	Chickweed	Lobelia
Bayberry	Comfrey	Marshmallow
Bee Pollen	Eyebright	Mullein
Burdock	Fenugreek	Parsley

Vitamins: A, C, E

HEADACHE (See also MIGRAINE HEADACHE)

(1)	**Fenugreek**	**Thyme**
(4)	Ginger	Vervain
Black Cohosh	Lobelia	Willow
Blessed Thistle	Passion Flower	Wintergreen
Brigham Tea	Pennyroyal	**Wood Betony**
Camomile	Peppermint	Yerba Santa
Catnip	Sage	

Black Cohosh is especially good for pains in back of head.

Vitamins: B
Minerals: Calcium

HEART

(4)	Blue Cohosh	**Hawthorn**
(13)	**Cayenne**	Horsetail
Barberry	Garlic	Lobelia
Black Cohosh	Golden Seal	Mistletoe

Oat Straw	Saffron (Safflowers)	Valerian
Rose Hips	Shepherd's Purse	Wood Betony
Rue	St. Johnswort	

Shepherd's Purse normalizes heart action. Lobelia helps heart palpitations.

Vitamins: B, C, E, Lecithin

Minerals: Calcium, Magnesium, Potassium

HEARTBURN

(4)	Rue	Wood Betony
(30)	Saffron (Safflowers)	Wormwood
Barberry	Sarsaparilla	Enzymes are also
Fenugreek	Thyme	beneficial
Peppermint	Valerian	

Vitamins: B

HEMORRHAGE

Bowels:
Mullein

External:

Bistort	Echinacea	Slippery Elm
Camomile	Golden Seal	St. Johnswort
Cayenne	Horsetail	White Oak Bark
Comfrey	Papaya	Willow
Dandelion	**Plantain**	Yerba Santa

Internal:

Bayberry	Ginseng	St. Johnswort
Bistort	**Golden Seal**	**White Oak Bark**
Cayenne	Plantain	Willow
Comfrey	Shepherd's Purse	Yarrow

Bistort, Golden Seal, and White Oak Bark can be used as Douche, Enema, or can be snuffed up the nose.

Lungs:

| Bayberry | Ginger | Yarrow |
| Cayenne | **Mullein** | |

Nose:

| Brigham Tea | **Golden Seal** | **White Oak Bark** |

Urinary:

Comfrey	Nettle	White Oak Bark
Marshmallow		

Uterine:

Bayberry	False Unicorn	**Mistletoe**

Vaginal:

Bistort	**White Oak Bark**	Witch Hazel
Golden Seal		

Marshmallow can be used for bladder hemorrhage by simmering 1 oz. of Marshmallow in 1 pint of milk and drinking ½ cup each ½ hour. For bowel hemorrhage: 1 oz. Mullein to 1 pint of milk simmered slowly and drink 1 pint every bowel movement. Lemon Juice diluted and taken cold is also good for internal hemorrhage.
Vitamins: C, E, K

HEMORRHOIDS & PILES

Aloe Vera	Golden Seal	Uva Ursi
Buckthorn	Mullein	**White Oak Bark**
Burdock	Plantain	Witch Hazel
Camomile	Poke Root	Yarrow
Cascara Sagrada	Psyllium	
Chickweed	Shepherd's Purse	

Golden Seal and White Oak Bark packs help to alleviate the pain. Put vitamin E on a piece of peeled, raw potato the size of a little finger and insert at night to reduce swelling and pain in hemorrhoids.
Vitamins: A, B, C, E, Lecithin
Minerals: Potassium

HEPATITIS (See LIVER)

HERPES

Black Walnut

HIGH BLOOD PRESSURE (see BLOOD PRESSURE)

HOARSENESS

(21)	Comfrey	Golden Seal
Bayberry	Fennel	Hops
Chickweed	Fenugreek	Horseradish

Hyssop	Marshmallow	Sage
Licorice Root	Mullein	Slippery Elm
Lobelia	Plantain	Yerba Santa

Any of the above herbs are good as a gargle or tea.
Vitamins: C, E

HORMONE IMBALANCE

Female:

(8)	Black Cohosh	Damiana
(32)	**Blessed Thistle**	Sarsaparilla

Male:

(26)	Ginseng	**Sarsaparilla**
(32)		

Ginseng and Sarsaparilla taken together are very helpful in balancing male hormones.

HOT FLASHES

(8)	Black Cohosh	Kelp
(32)	**Damiana**	Sarsaparilla

HYPERACTIVITY

(4)	(6)	**Lobelia**

Avoid all artificial flavoring and food coloring.
Vitamins: B Complex
Minerals: Massive doses of all minerals

HYPOGLYCEMIA

(4)	Catnip	Lobelia
15)	Dandelion	Marshmallow
(25)	Juniper	**Saffron (Safflowers)**
Black Cohosh	Kelp	Scullcap
Blue Cohosh	**Licorice Root**	Valerian Root

Some people who have Hypoglycemia can not handle Golden Seal as it tends to lower the blood sugar. Saffron (Safflowers) is good to take before exercising.
Vitamins: B, C, E, Pantothenic Acid
Minerals: Magnesium, Potassium

HYSTERIA

(4)	Camomile	Scullcap
(6)	Catnip	St. Johnswort
(14)	**Lobelia**	Valerian
Black Cohosh	**Mistletoe**	
Blue Cohosh	Rue	

Vitamins: B
Minerals: Calcium

IMPOTENCY (See FRIGIDITY)

INDIGESTION (See also DIGESTION)

(14)	Fennel	Papaya
(30)	Fenugreek	Parsley
Barberry	Garlic	Peppermint
Bayberry	Ginseng	**Saffron (Safflowers)**
Blessed Thistle	Golden Seal	Sage
Camomile	Hops	Scullcap
Cascara Sagrada	Horseradish	Thyme
Cayenne	Hyssop	Valerian Root
Comfrey	Lobelia	Wood Betony
Dandelion	Myrrh	Wormwood
Eyebright	Oat Straw	

Vitamins: B

INFECTION

(3)	(24)	Golden Seal
(16)	Cayenne	
(17)	Echinacea	

External:

| (24) | Comfrey | Poke Weed |
| Cayenne | Garlic | |

Cayenne and Garlic douche for uterus.
Vitamins: A, C, E

INFLAMMATION & SWELLING (See also BRUISES)

(3)	Golden Seal	Slippery Elm
Chickweed	Hyssop	Wood Betony
Comfrey	Marshmallow	Yellow Dock
Ginseng	Poke Root	Yerba Santa

Comfrey and Wood Betony are good for sprains. Onion packs are also good.
Vitamins: A, C, E

INSANITY

(6)	Catnip	Rue
(12)	Lobelia	Scullcap
(14)	Peppermint	Wood Betony

Vitamins: B

INSECT BITES (See BEE STINGS & BITES)

Rue repels flies and other insects.

INSOMNIA

(4)	Hawthorn	Peppermint
(14)	Hops	Scullcap
Catnip	Mullein	Valerian
Dandelion	Passion Flower	

Vitamins: B
Minerals: Calcium, Iron

INTESTINES (See COLON, CONSTIPATION, DIARRHEA, DYSENTERY)

ITCHING (See also ECZEMA, SKIN DISEASE)

(3)	**Chickweed**	Peppermint
Buckthorn	Golden Seal	Plantain
Burdock	Pennyroyal	**Yellow Dock**

Peppermint tea bath is very beneficial.
Vitamins: B

JAUNDICE

(3)	Dandelion	Parsley
(4)	Fennel	Rose Hips
(22)	Hops	Senna
Barberry	Horsetail	St. Johnswort
Camomile	Irish Moss	White Oak Bark
Cascara Sagrada	Lobelia	Yarrow
Cayenne	Oat Straw	

Vitamins: B, C, E

JOINTS (See also ARTHRITIS, GOUT, RHEUMATISM)

| (4) | Horseradish | Rue |
| Burdock | Mullein | |

Vitamins: A, C, E
Minerals: Calcium, Magnesium

KIDNEYS (See also BLADDER, URINATION)

(18)	Catnip	Oat Straw
(19)	Cayenne	**Parsley**
Alfalfa	Chaparral	Plantain
Barberry	Comfrey	Queen of the Meadow
Black Cohosh	Dandelion	Rose Hips
Blessed Thistle	Golden Seal	Shepherd's Purse
Blue Cohosh	Hyssop	**Uva Ursi**
Brigham Tea	Juniper	White Oak Bark
Burdock	Kelp	Wood Betony
Camomile	Marshmallow	Yarrow

Vitamins: A, B, C, E
Minerals: Magnesium

LABOR (See AFTER PAINS, CHILDBIRTH, PREGNANCY)

LACTATION

Enrich:
(4)   **Blessed Thistle**

Promote:
| Blessed Thistle | **Marshmallow** | Raspberry |
| Fennel | | |

Slow Down:
Black Walnut Bark   **Parsley**   **Sage**

Add Papaya to cows milk to resemble breast milk.

Minerals: Calcium, Manganese, Phosphorus

LARYNGITIS (See HOARSENESS)

LEUCORRHEA

Bayberry	False Unicorn	Slippery Elm
Black Walnut	**Golden Seal**	Uva Ursi
Blessed Thistle	Myrrh	**White Oak Bark**
Blue Cohosh	Plantain	
Comfrey	Raspberry	

Vitamins: A, C, E

LIVER (See also JAUNDICE)

(3)	Garlic	Parsley
(4)	Gentian	Peppermint
(22)	Golden Seal	Poke Weed
Barberry	Hops	Senna
Black Cohosh	Horseradish	Uva Ursi
Blessed Thistle	Horsetail	White Oak Bark
Buckthorn	Hyssop	Wormwood
Burdock	Lobelia	Yellow Dock
Cascara Sagrada	Mandrake	Yarrow
Dandelion	Oat Straw	

Vitamins: A, B, C, E

LOCK JAW (See TETANUS)

LONGEVITY (See also VITALITY)

(12)	**Ginseng**	Sarsaparilla
Damiana	**Gotu Kola**	
False Unicorn	Licorice	

Vitamins: A, B, C, E

LOW BLOOD PRESSURE (See BLOOD PRESSURE)

71

LOW BLOOD SUGAR (See HYPOGLYCEMIA)

LUMBAGO (Lower Back Pain. See also CRAMPS; Leg & Muscle, RHEUMATISM)

(4)	Juniper	Poke Root
(24)	Oat Straw	Queen of the Meadow
Bayberry	Parsley	Uva Ursi
Black Cohosh	Plantain	

Vitamins: B, E
Minerals: Calcium

LUNGS (See also EMPHYSEMA, PNEUMONIA)

(21)	Horseradish	Pleurisy Root
Bayberry	Hyssop	Sage
Black Cohosh	Licorice	Shepherd's Purse
Blessed Thistle	Lobelia	Slippery Elm
Chickweed	Marshmallow	St. Johnswort
Comfrey	**Mullein**	Thyme
Eucalyptus	Myrrh	Yarrow
Fenugreek	Oat Straw	Yerba Santa
Ginger	Pennyroyal	
Ginseng	Plantain	

Vitamins: A, C, E

LUPUS (See also, ARTHRITIS, JOINTS, SKIN DISEASE)

(2)	**(4)**	Black Walnut
(3)		

Vitamins: A, B, C, E
Minerals: Calcium, Magnesium

LYMPH & SWOLLEN GLANDS

(3)	**Echinacea**	Poke Root
(16)	Golden Seal	Saw Palmetto
(17)	Mullein	

Exercise is probably one of the most important things that can be done to help lymph move through the body.

Saw Palmetto helps to strengthen the glands.
Vitamins: A, C, E, Pantothenic Acid

MEASLES (See also CONTAGIOUS DISEASES)

Camomile	Peppermint	Shepherd's Purse
Catnip	Pleurisy Root	Valerian
Golden Seal	Raspberry	Vervain
Hyssop	Rue	Yarrow
Lobelia	Saffron (Safflowers)	

Valerian is helpful for restlessness.
Vitamins: C
(See *Herbalist Magazine*, Volume 1 #1)

MENOPAUSE

(6)	**Damiana**	Licorice
(8)	Gotu Kola	Rue
(32)	Hawthorn	Sarsaparilla
Black Cohosh	Kelp	Shepherd's Purse

Rue will help heart palpitations. Black Cohosh acts as a natural estrogen.
Vitamins: A, B, C, E

MENSTRUATION

Cramps: (See CRAMPS)

Difficulties:

(4)	Catnip	Parsley
(8)	Cramp Bark	Wild Yam
Black Cohosh	Hops	Yarrow
Blue Cohosh	Myrrh	

Excessive:

(8)	Golden Seal	Uva Ursi
Bayberry	Marshmallow	White Oak Bark
Bistort	**Mistletoe**	Wood Betony
Cayenne	Plantain	Yarrow
Comfrey	Raspberry	
False Unicorn	Shepherd's Purse	

Suppressed:

(8)	Ginger	Sage
Black Cohosh	Parsley	Squaw Vine
Blue Cohosh	Pennyroyal	St. Johnswort
Brigham Tea	Peppermint	Thyme
Camomile	Pleurisy Root	Valerian
Catnip	Rue	Vervain
Fennel	Saffron (Safflowers)	Wild Yam

Vitamins: B, C, E

MIGRAINE HEADACHES (See also HEADACHES)

(4)	Garlic	Shepherd's Purse
Blessed Thistle	Hops	**Thyme**
Cayenne	**Lobelia**	Valerian
Fennel	Peppermint	Wood Betony
Fenugreek	Rosemary	

Thyme used with Fenugreek is very helpful, also used with Wood Betony. Migraine Headaches come from various problems: diet, neck problems, deficiencies, nerves, stress, etc.
Vitamins: B
Minerals: Calcium

MILK (See LACTATION)

MISCARRIAGE

Bayberry	False Unicorn	**Lobelia**
Catnip		

Vitamins: E

MORNING SICKNESS (See also NAUSEA, VOMITING)

(8)	Golden Seal	**Raspberry**
(11)	Hops	Sage
Alfalfa	Kelp	Wild Yam
Catnip	Peach Leaves	
Ginger	Peppermint	

Vitamins: B, E

74

MOUTH SORES (See also THRUSH, ULCERS)

Barberry	**Golden Seal**	Sage
Bistort	Myrrh	**White Oak Bark**
Chickweed	**Raspberry**	Yerba Santa

Raspberry is for cankers.
Vitamins: C, E

MUCOUS MEMBRANES & MUCOUS (See also SINUS)

(5)	Golden Seal	Pleurisy Root
(10)	Horseradish	Raspberry
(16)	Horsetail	Sarsaparilla
(17)	Hyssop	**Thyme**
(21)	Juniper	Uva Ursi
Bayberry	Lobelia	Witch Hazel
Comfrey	Marshmallow	Yarrow
Fennel	Mullein	Yerba Santa
Fenugreek	Pennyroyal	

Vitamins: A, C, E

MULTIPLE SCLEROSIS

(4)	(28)	Black Walnut
(19)		

Although the herbs are helpful, it seems that diet is more important.
Lecithin seems to be helpful also.
Vitamins: B, C, E; a natural multivitamin-mineral is important.

MUMPS (See also CONTAGIOUS DISEASES)

Cayenne	Ginger	Scullcap
Mullein		

(See *Herbalist Magazine*, Volume 1 #1)

NAUSEA (See also MORNING SICKNESS, VOMITING)

(4)	Ginger	Sage
(11)	Pennyroyal	Spearmint
Alfalfa	Peppermint	Wild Yam
Golden Seal	**Raspberry**	

Vitamins: B
Minerals: Calcium

NEPHRITIS (See KIDNEY)

NERVES

(4)	Hops	Raspberry
(6)	Horsetail	**Red Clover**
(14)	Lettuce	Rue
Black Cohosh	**Lobelia**	Sage
Blue Cohosh	Marshmallow	Scullcap
Burdock	Mistletoe	Squaw Vine
Camomile	Myrrh	St. Johnswort
Cascara Sagrada	Oat Straw	Thyme
Catnip	Passion Flower	Valerian
Celery	Peach Leaves	Vervain
Ginger	Pennyroyal	Wood Betony
Goldenseal	Peppermint	
Hawthorn	Queen of the Meadow	

Vitamins: B
Minerals: Calcium, Iodine, Magnesium, Sodium

NIGHTMARES

(4)	Catnip	Thyme
(6)	Hops	
(14)	Peppermint	

Vitamins: B
Minerals: Calcium

NIGHT SWEATS

Hops	Nettle	Strawberry Leaves
Hyssop	Sage	Yarrow

NURSING (See also BREASTS, LACTATION)

Caked Breasts: (See BREASTS)

Horseradish will help clear the nasal passages in nursing babies if allowed to breath the fumes.

76

OBESITY

(4)	Chaparral	Hops
(27)	**Chickweed**	Irish Moss
(29)	Fennel	Kelp
Burdock	Golden Seal	Uva Ursi

(27) can be taken with Chickweed. Start slowly as the (27) will help to cleanse the system. If too much is taken at once diarrhea may occur, as this cleansing takes place. If weight loss is too slow, add more Chickweed.
Vitamins: B, C, E, Lecithin
Minerals: Calcium

PAIN (See also AFTERPAIN, CRAMPS, HEADACHE, MIGRAINE HEADACHE)

(1)	**Lobelia**	Wild Lettuce
(4)	Marshmallow	Wild Yam
(14)	Poke Root	Wood Betony
Catnip	Valerian	

Vitamins: C
Minerals: Calcium

PALSY

(4)	Cayenne	Valerian
(6)	**Lobelia**	Wood Betony
(14)	Sage	

Vitamins: B
Minerals: Calcium

PANCREAS

(3)	Buchu	Golden Seal
(22)	Cayenne	**Juniper**
(23)	Comfrey	Uva Ursi
Blueberries	Dandelion	

PARALYSIS (See Cleansing Chapter)

(14)	Eucalyptus	Scullcap
Black Cohosh	Ginger	Valerian
Cayenne	Oat Straw	Yellow Dock

Vitamins: B, C,
Minerals: Iron, Phosphorus

PARASITES

(20)
(28)
Black Walnut
Buckthorn
Camomile
Catnip
Garlic
Hops
Horseradish
Hyssop
Onion
Papaya
Pumpkin
Sage
Senna
Valerian
White Oak Bark
Wood Betony
Wormwood

Raisins soaked in Senna tea are helpful in expelling parasites. Enemas should be used when taking (28). Small children can eat Pumpkin Seeds.

PARKINSON'S DISEASE

(19)
(32)
Cayenne
Damiana
Ginseng

Although this illness is one that probably needs medical attention, Diet, Nutrition and Cleansing play a great part, as do the herbs, to help relieve some of the symptoms.
Vitamins: B, C, E; A natural multivitamin-mineral.
Minerals: Calcium, Magnesium

PERSPIRATION

Excessive:
Wood Betony

Odors:
Horsetail (foot bath)

Produce:
Ginger
Hyssop
Pennyroyal
Pleurisy Root
Yarrow

A Ginger bath will help produce perspiration and clean the pores in any type of illness, especially good for colds and flu.

PILES (See HEMORRHOIDS & PILES)

PITUITARY GLAND

(12)	Alfalfa	Kelp
(19)	**Ginseng**	Parsley
(29)	**Gotu Kola**	Yellow Dock

Vitamins: C, E, Lecithin

PLEURISY (See also LUNGS, PNEUMONIA)

(4)	**Lobelia**	**Slippery Elm**
Cayenne	**Mullein**	Yarrow
Chickweed	Pleurisy Root	

½ teaspoon Cayenne, 1 Tablespoon Lobelia, and 3 Tablespoons Slippery Elm. Mix with mineral water. Leave on chest only one hour.
Vitamins: A, C, E
Minerals: Calcium

PNEUMONIA (See also LUNGS)

(16)	Fenugreek	Marshmallow
(17)	Ginger	**Mullein**
(21)	Irish Moss	Pleurisy Root
Comfrey	**Lobelia**	

Poultice of:	4 capsules Lobelia
	1 capsule Quinine
	1 tsp. Oil of Turpentine

Mix with mentholatum, vaseline, or vicks. Put on cloth on chest.

Vitamins: A, C, E

POISON IVY & OAK

Aloe Vera	**Burdock**	**Mullein**
Black Walnut	Lobelia	**Yellow Dock**

Within 10 foot radius of the Poison Ivy or Oak, there will be something to counteract the poison: one of the above herbs. Rub the leaf on the affected part. This must be done immediately.
Corn Starch has been known to help the itching temporarily by applying a paste on the area. **Tincture of Black Walnut** will help the itching. Aloe Vera gel as a wash is also used for itching. The system needs to be cleansed with enemas.

79

Vitamins: **High doses of C.**

POISONING

Blood:
| (3) | Echinacea | Plantain |
| Chickweed | | |

Food:
Lobelia

Ptomaine:
Eat two heads Iceburg Lettuce.

Lobelia will cause vomiting if taken in large doses. For this reason, it is used for food poisoning to empty the stomach.
Vitamins: A, C, E

PREGNANCY (See also AFTERPAIN, BIRTH DEFECTS, CHILD-BIRTH)

| (4) | **Raspberry** | Kelp |

Complications:
False Unicorn

Do Not Use During Pregnancy:
| Pennyroyal | Rue |

Vitamins: B, E; A natural multivitamin-mineral
Minerals: Manganese

PROSTATE

(26)	Garlic	Queen of the Meadow
Bee Pollen	Ginseng	Rosemary
Buchu	Golden Seal	Saw Palmetto
Chaparral	Juniper	Uva Ursi
Damiana	Kelp	
Echinacea	Parsley	

Vitamins: B, C, E
Minerals: **Zinc**

PSORIASIS

(3)	Chickweed	Kelp
(4)	Comfrey	Red Clover
Aloe Vera	Dandelion	Saffron (Safflowers)
Burdock	Golden Seal	Sarsaparilla
Chaparral	Jojoba Shampoo	Yellow Dock

Head:
Jojoba Shampoo can also be used on the body.

Aloe Vera used internally as well as externally.
Vitamins: A, B, C, E, Lecithin
Minerals: Calcium, Magnesium

PYORRHEA (See also MOUTH SORES)

(30)	**Golden Seal**	**White Oak Bark**
Cayenne	Myrrh	

Vitamins: A, B, C, E

RABIES

Cayenne	Lobelia	Scullcap
Garlic		

Vitamins: C, E

RESPIRATORY (See LUNGS)

RHEUMATIC REVER (See also CONTAGIOUS DISEASES, FEVER, JOINTS)

(16)	(22)	Pleurisy Root
(17)	Lobelia	

Vitamins: A, B, C, E

RHEUMATISM (See also ARTHRITIS, GOUT)

(1)	(24)	Black Cohosh
(2)	**Alfalfa**	Brigham Tea
(4)	Barberry	Buchu

Buckthorn　　　　　Hawthorn　　　　　Red Clover
Burdock　　　　　Hops　　　　　　　Rue
Cayenne　　　　　　Horseradish　　　　Sarsaparilla
Chaparral　　　　Lobelia　　　　　　Scullcap
Chickweed　　　　　Oat Straw　　　　　Willow
Comfrey　　　　　　Poke Weed　　　　　Yerba Santa
Fennel　　　　　　　Queen of the Meadow
Garlic　　　　　　　Raspberry

Vitamins: C, E
Minerals: Calcium, Magnesium

RINGWORM

(3)　　　　　　　　Golden Seal　　　　Poke Root
Black Walnut　　　Lobelia　　　　　　Sarsaparilla

Apply apple cider vinegar to skin, or use Black Walnut tincture.

SCALDS (See BURNS)

SCARLET FEVER (See also CONTAGIOUS DISEASES)

Bayberry　　　　　　Myrrh　　　　　　　Yellow Dock
Brigham Tea　　　　Red Clover
Lobelia　　　　　　Valerian Root

Vitamins: A, C, E
(See *Herbalist Magazine*, Volume 1 #1)

SCIATICA

(4)　　　　　　　　Fenugreek　　　　　Rue
(6)　　　　　　　　Horseradish

Use Horseradish as a poultice.
Vitamins: B
Minerals: Calcium

SENILITY (See also AGE SPOTS, VITALITY)

(12)　　　　　　　Dandelion　　　　　**Gotu Kola**
(19)　　　　　　　　False Unicorn　　　Licorice
Damiana　　　　　　Ginseng　　　　　　Sarsaparilla

Vitamins: A, B, C, E

82

SEX DESIRE (See FRIGIDITY, STERILITY)

Decrease:
(14)	Sage	Willow
Hops	Scullcap	

Increase:
(32)	Ginseng	Saffron (Safflowers)
Damiana	Licorice	Slippery Elm

Vitamins: E

SHINGLES (See also SKIN DISEASE)

(6)	Peppermint	Thyme

Apple Cider Vinegar may be applied topically. Use thyme as a salve.
Apply Oil of Peppermint externally.
Vitamins: B, C, Lecithin
Minerals: Calcium, Magnesium

SHOCK

(13)	Ginger	Myrrh
Cayenne	**Lobelia**	Valerian

Vitamins: C, E

SINUS (See also MUCOUS MEMBRANE)

(10)	**Comfrey**	Horseradish
(20)	Fennel	Hyssop
(21)	**Fenugreek**	Mullein
Bayberry	Garlic	Witch Hazel
Brigham Tea	Ginger	
Cayenne	Golden Seal	

Bayberry, Brigham Tea, and Golden Seal may be snuffed up the nose mixed or individually. Another good remedy is to boil 1 pint water and add 1 teaspoon of salt and 1 teaspoon of soda, cool and add 1 Tablespoon Witch Hazel and use this solution to snuff up the nose and spit out. Do this several times a day.
Vitamins: A, C, Pantothenic Acid

SKIN DISEASE (See also ACNE, ECZEMA)

(3)	Dandelion	Red Clover
Barberry	Ginger Baths	Redmond Clay
Black Cohosh	Golden Seal	Sage
Black Walnut	Horseradish	White Oak Bark
Brigham Tea	Hyssop	**Yellow Dock**
Buckthorn	Mullein	Yarrow
Burdock	Pennyroyal	
Chickweed	Poke Root	

Vitamins: A, B, C, Niacin

SLEEP (See INSOMNIA)

SMOKING (See also COUGH, see Cleansing Chapter)

(3)	Catnip	Scullcap
(21)	Echinacea	Slippery Elm
Black Cohosh	Magnolia	Valerian
Blue Cohosh	Peppermint	

Vitamins: C

SORES (See WOUNDS)

SORE THROAT (See THROAT)

SPLEEN

(3)	Cayenne	Vervain
(22)	Dandelion	Yellow Dock
Barberry	Horseradish	Yarrow
Camomile	Parsley	
Cascara Sagrada	Uva Ursi	

Vitamins: C

SPRAINS (See also INFLAMMATION)

Onion Packs

The author does not directly or indirectly dispense medical advice or prescribe the use of herbs as a form of treatment for sickness without medical approval.

STERILITY (See also FRIGIDITY)

(8)   (32)   False Unicorn
(12)

Vitamins: E

STOMACH (See also ULCERS)

(4)	Fennel	Papaya
(30)	Fenugreek	**Peppermint**
Alfalfa	Garlic	Plantain
Bayberry	Ginger	Raspberry
Blessed Thistle	Ginseng	Rue
Burdock	**Golden Seal**	Sage
Camomile	Hops	Spearmint
Carob	Hyssop	**Slippery Elm**
Catnip	Juniper	Thyme
Cayenne	Licorice	Valerian
Chickweed	Myrrh	Wormwood
Comfrey	Nettle	

STONES (See GALL STONES, GRAVEL & STONES, KIDNEY)

STRESS (See NERVES)

ST. VITUS DANCE (See also NERVES)

(6)   Black Cohosh   **Lobelia**
(14)

Vitamins: B

SUNBURN (See BURNS)

SUN STROKE

Pennyroyal

Vitamins: C, E

SWELLING (See INFLAMMATION & SWELLING)

SYPHILLIS (See VENERAL DISEASE)

TEETH

Decayed:
(4)   Alfalfa

Loose:
Pomegranate   **White Oak Bark Tea**

Stained:
Black Walnut   Myrrh

Toothache:

(1)	Hyssop	Pennyroyal
(4)	**Lobelia**	White Oak Bark
Cloves	Mullein	
Hops	Myrrh	

Brush teeth with Black Walnut Powder to help remove stains.
Vitamins: A, C
Minerals: Calcium, Magneisum, Phosphorus

TETANUS

(12)   Cayenne   Lobelia

Use Lobelia tincture.
Vitamins: C

THROAT (See also HOARSENESS)

(16)	Comfrey	Mullein
(17)	Fenugreek	Myrrh
(29)	Golden Seal	Pineapple
Bayberry	**Horehound**	Raspberry
Barberry	Hyssop	Sage
Burdock	Juniper	Slippery Elm
Cayenne	**Licorice**	White Oak Bark
Chickweed	Marshmallow	

A towel wrung out of salt water applied around the neck will help a sore throat. Place plastic over the towel to keep the pillow dry.
Vitamins: A, C, E

THRUSH (See also MOUTH SORES)

(30)	Plantain	**White Oak Bark**
Myrrh	Rue	

Vitamins: A, C, E

THYROID

(29)	**Irish Moss**	Parsley
Black Cohosh	**Kelp**	**Poke Root**

Low:

Bayberry	Golden Seal	Myrrh

Vitamins: C, E
Minerals: Iodine

TONGUE (See MOUTH)

TONSILLITIS

(5)	Echinacea	White Oak Bark
(16)	Golden Seal	Wood Betony
(17)	Sage	
Comfrey	Slippery Elm	

Mix Glycerine and Iodine until it is a deep amber color, then use as a swab or a gargle to help the swelling. An enema will help to clean out the colon and help get rid of the infection.
Vitamins: A, C, E, Pantothenic Acid

TOOTHACHES (See TEETH)

TUBERCULOSIS (See LUNGS)

TUMORS (See also CANCER)

(3)	Chickweed	Plantain
(28)	Lobelia	Poke Root
Chaparral	Mullein	Yellow Dock

A poultice of 3 parts Mullein to 1 part Lobelia will help the sweeling.

TYPHOID (See CONTAGIOUS DISEASES)

ULCERS (See also STOMACH)

(4)	Fenugreek	Plantain
(30)	Garlic	Psyllium
Alfalfa	Golden Seal	Raspberry
Bayberry	Hops	Sage
Burdock	Licorice	Slippery Elm
Chickweed	Myrrh	Valerian
Comfrey	Pennyroyal	White Oak Bark

Leg Ulcers: See WOUNDS

Vitamins: B, C, E
Minerals: Calcium

URINATION (See BLADDER, KIDNEYS)

Bloody:

Comfrey	Marshmallow	White Oak Bark

Difficulties:

Queen of the Meadow	Squaw Vine	St. Johnswort
Slippery Elm		

Increases:

Burdock	Dandelion	Yarrow
Catnip	Fennel	

Urethral Irritation:

Buchu	Golden Seal

For bloody urination, see HEMORRHAGE.
Vitamins: A, C, E

UTERUS

(8)	Golden Seal	Raspberry
Black Cohosh	Myrrh	Wild Yam
Catnip	Queen of the Meadow	Yarrow
False Unicorn		

See directions at beginning of chapter.

Prolapsed:

Bayberry   Uva Ursi   White Oak Bark
False Unicorn

Vitamins: E

VAGINA (See also DOUCHE)

(8)	Ginger	Queen of the Meadow
Barberry	Golden Seal	Shepherd's Purse
Black Walnut	Magnolia	Slippery Elm
Blue Cohosh	Marshmallow	Uva Ursi
False Unicorn	Myrrh	White Oak Bark
Fenugreek	Plantain	

Vitamins: A, C, E

VARICOSE VEINS (See also CIRCULATION)

(4)	Cayenne	Witch Hazel
Bayberry	White Oak Bark	Wood Betony

White Oak Bark can be taken internally. Also steeped as a tea for external packs applied to veins.

VENERAL DISEASES

(3)	Echinacea	Wintergreen
Black Walnut	Golden Seal	Witch Hazel
Burdock	Uva Ursi	Yellow Dock

These herbs can be taken internally and used in tea form for douches.
Vitamins: A, B, C, E

VITALITY (See also ENDURANCE, ENERGY)

(12)	Dandelion	**Licorice**
(13)	Gotu Kola	Yellow Dock

Vitamins: C, E
Minerals: Iron

VOICE (See HOARSENESS)

VOMITING (See also MORNING SICKNESS, NAUSEA)

(11)   Peach Leaves

Vitamins: B

WARTS

Buckthorn	Garlic	Milkweed
Chaparral	Mandrake	Mullein

The milk from the Milkweed is good. Also, Vitamin E, and Castor Oil have helped in many cases.
Vitamins: A, C, E

WATER RETENTION

(4)	Fenugreek	**Peach Bark**
(18)	Golden Seal	Pleurisy
(19)	Hops	Queen of the Meadow
Blue Cohosh	Horsetail	**Saffron (Safflowers)**
Dandelion	Juniper	Shepherd's Purse
Fennel	**Parsley**	Slippery Elm

Vitamins: B, C,
Minerals: Calcium, Potassium

WHOOPING COUGH (See also COUGH)

Ginseng	Mullein	Thyme

Vitamins: C

WORMS (See PARASITES)

WOUNDS

(3)	Camomile	Golden Seal
(4)	Cayenne	Horsetail
(24)	Chaparral	Lobelia
(30)	Chickweed	Myrrh
Aloe Vera	Comfrey	Papaya
Bayberry	Dandelion	Peach Bark
Bistort	Echinacea	Plantain

Slippery Elm	Willow	Yerba Santa
St. Johnswort	Witch Hazel	
Vervain	Wood Betony	

These herbs can be used internally and also as poultices (See Definitions and Directions Chapter).
Vitamins: A, B, C, E
Minerals: Calcium

YEAST INFECTION

Cayenne	Garlic

Fresh Garlic as a douche will usually clean it up in 3 days.
Vitamins: A, C, E

Chapter 5

PREGNANCIES, BABIES, AND NURSING

The author does not directly or indirectly dispense medical advice or prescribe the use of herbs as a form of treatment for sickness without medical approval. Nutritionists and other experts in the field of health and nutrition hold widely varying views. It is not the intent of the author to diagnose or prescribe. Our intent is only to offer health information to help you cooperate with your doctor in your mutual problem of building health. In the event you use this information without your doctor's approval, you are prescribing for yourself, which is your constitutional right, but the publisher assumes no responsibility.

PREGNANCY

Proper Diet is one of the most important and valuable practices during pregnancy. It should consist mostly of fresh fruits and vegetables with some whole grain cereals and nuts.

Kelp, Raspberry, and Vitamin E are all very important. If they are taken throughout the pregnancy, the possibilities of birth defects and mental retardation are greatly decreased. They will also aid in the labor and delivery process.

(19) helps provide energy and also contains all of the vitamins and minerals that the body needs.

(4) is very high in calcium and silicon which are important in building good bones and teeth in the baby and providing the mother with sufficient calcium for herself. It should be taken in abundance, especially during the last month of pregnancy.

The pregnant woman can use (33) during the last five or six weeks to help strengthen the uterus and make her delivery much easier. This seems to prepare all of the female organs and get them ready for childbirth.

CAUTION: The following herbs should not be used during pregnancy: (28), Pennyroyal, Rue, or any laxative herbs.

BABIES

Powdered herbs can be put in applesauce, molasses, or honey. Capsulated herbs can be inserted in the baby's rectum.

1. **Colic:** Catnip, Fennel, Peppermint, or any combination of these three, in a tea. Honey is also helpful.

2. **Constipation:** Licorice Root Tea, or honey.

3. **Diaper Rash:** Mullein Leaf, Slippery Elm (used internally in juice) or apply as paste.

4. **Diarrhea:** Slippery Elm enema (½ teaspoon to 1 cup water) 1 teaspoon carob powder or Slippery Elm to 1 cup boiled skim milk.

5. **Fever:** Catnip tea enema, Raspberry leaf tea.

6. **Loss of Appetite:** Camomile Tea.

7. **Pinworms:** Camomile Tea.

8. **Restless:** Hops Tea, 1 teaspoon tincture of Lobelia rubbed on baby's spine will settle him down as it helps to relax. You can also give the baby a few drops of the tincture.

9. **Teething:** Rub tincture of Lobelia on gums.

Tea is made by putting 1 teaspoon herb in 1 cup boiling water, covering, and after 10 minutes straining. Honey can be added for taste.

NURSING

Blessed Thistle, Fennel, or Marshmallow taken hot will bring in good rich milk. This will sustain the baby longer and help him sleep through the night at an earlier age.

Parsley or Sage will help dry up the milk when the mother is ready to quit nursing.

Poke Root packs will help alleviate caked breasts.

If the baby has an infection, the mother can take vitamin C and (17), or other vitamins and herbs and the baby will receive them through the milk.

CAUTION: If the nursing mother is taking too many cleansing herbs it may cause colic or diarrhea in the baby.

Chapter 6

VITAMIN AND MINERAL SOURCES

Vitamin A

Alfalfa, Burdock, Cayenne, Dandelion, Garlic, Kelp, Marshmallow, Papaya, Parsley, Pokeweed, Raspberry, Red Clover, Saffron, Watercress, Yellow Dock.

Vitamin B_1
(Thiamine)

Cayenne, Dandelion, Fenugreek, Kelp, Parsley, Raspberry.

Vitamin B_2
(Riboflavin)

Alfalfa, Burdock, Dandelion, Fenugreek, Kelp Parsley, Saffron, Watercress.

Vitamin B_3
(Niacin)

Alfalfa, Burdock, Dandelion, Fenugreek, Kelp, Parsley, Sage.

Vitamin B_6
(Pyridoxine)

Alfalfa.

Vitamin B_{12}
(Cyanocobalamin; Cobalt)

Alfalfa, Kelp.

Vitamin C

Alfalfa, Burdock, Boneset, Catnip, Cayenne, Chickweed, Dandelion, Garlic, Hawthorn, Horseradish, Kelp, Lobelia, Parsley, Plantain, Pokeweed, Papaya, Raspberry, Rose Hips, Shepherd's Purse, Strawberry, Watercress, Yellow Dock.

Vitamin D

Alfalfa, Watercress.

Vitamin E

Alfalfa, Dandelion, Kelp, Raspberry, Rose Hips, Watercress.

Vitamin G

Alfalfa, Cayenne, Dandelion, Gotu Kola, Kelp.

Vitamin K	Alfalfa, Plantain, Shepherd's Purse.
Vitamin P (Rutin)	Dandelion, Rose Hips, Rue.
Vitamin T	Plantain.
Vitamin U (For Peptic Ulcers)	Alfalfa.
Aluminum	Alfalfa.
Calcium	Alfalfa, Blue Cohosh, Camomile, Cayenne, Dandelion, Horsetail, Irish Moss, Kelp, Mistletoe, Nettle, Parsley, Plantain, Pokeweed, Raspberry, Rose Hips, Shepherd's Purse, Yellow Dock.
Chlorophyl	Alfalfa.
Chlorine	Alfalfa, Dandelion, Kelp, Parsley, Raspberry.
Copper	Kelp, Parsley.
Fluorine	Garlic.
Iodine	Dulse, Garlic, Irish Moss, Kelp, Sarsaparilla.
Iron	Alfalfa, Burdock, Blue Cohosh, Cayenne, Dandelion, Dulse, Kelp, Mullein, Nettle, Parsley, Pokeweed, Rhubarb, Rose Hips, Yellow Dock.
Lithium	Kelp.
Magnesium	Alfalfa, Blue Cohosh, Cayenne, Dandelion, Kelp, Mistletoe, Mullein, Peppermint, Primrose, Raspberry, Willow, Wintergreen.
Manganese	Kelp.
Phosphorus	Alfalfa, Blue Cohosh, Caraway, Cayenne, Chickweed, Dandelion, Garlic, Irish Moss, Kelp, Licorice, Parsley, Purslane, Pokeweed, Raspberry, Rose Hips, Watercress, Yellow Dock.

95

Potassium	Alfalfa, Blue Cohosh, Birch, Borage, Camomile, Coltsfoot, Comfrey, Centaury, Dandelion, Dulse, Eyebright, Fennel, Irish Moss, Kelp, Mistletoe, Mullein, Nettle, Papaya, Parsley, Peppermint, Plantain, Primrose, Raspberry, Shepherd's Purse, White Oak Bark, Wintergreen, Yarrow.
Selenium	Kelp.
Silicon	Alfalfa, Blue Cohosh, Burdock, Horsetail, Kelp, Nettle.
Sodium	Alfalfa, Dandelion, Dulse, Fennel, Irish Moss, Kelp, Mistletoe, Parsley, Shepherd's Purse, Willow.
Sulfur	Alfalfa, Burdock, Cayenne, Coltsfoot, Eyebright, Fennel, Garlic, Irish Moss, Kelp, Mullein, Nettle, Parsley, Plantain, Raspberry, Sage, Shepherd's Purse, Thyme.
Zinc	Kelp, Marshmallow.

Trace Minerals   Kelp.
(Boron, Bromine, Nickel, Strontium, Vanadium)

Chapter 7

POISONOUS PLANTS

Autumn Crocus. . . . . Bulb
Azaleas . . . . All parts
Black Locust . . . . Bark, Sprouts, Foliage
Buttercup . . . . All parts
Daffodil. . . . . Bulb
Elderberry. . . . . Shoots, Leaves, Bark
Fox Glove . . . . Leaves
Hyacinth. . . . . Bulb
Iris. . . . . Underground stems
Jack-in-the-Pulpit . . . . All parts
Jimson Weed. . . . . All parts
Larkspur . . . . Young plants, Seeds
Lily-of-the-Valley . . . . Leaves, Flowers
May Apple. . . . . .Apple, Foliage, Roots
Mistletoe. . . . . Berries
Monkshood. . . . . Fleshy roots
Moon Seed . . . . Berries
Narcissus. . . . . Bulb
Night Shade. All parts
Oaks . . . . Foliage, Acorns
Oleander . . . . Leaves, Branches
Poinsetta. . . . . Leaves
Poison Hemlock . . . . All parts
Poison Ivy. . . . . All parts
Potato. . . . . Leaves
Rhubarb . . . . Leaves, Blade
Star of Bethlehem . . . . Bulb
Water Hemlock . . . . All parts
Wild & Cultivated Cherries . . . . . . Twigs, Foliage
Wisteria. . . . . .Seeds, Pods

See *Nature's Medicine Chest* by LeArta Moulton
for colored pictures of these herbs.

Chapter 8

CLEANSING

In illness, the body has many ways of ridding itself of toxins. Mucous is expelled from the sinuses in the form of a runny nose, from the lungs by coughing. Toxins are eliminated through the colon by diarrhea, and the stomach, by vomiting.

This is all part of the cleansing process. We can help this process by diet, fasting, enemas, exercise, and a healthy mental attitude.

DIET

The purpose of a cleanse is to eliminate excessive mucous and toxins from the body. Animal protein, white flour, and white sugar are all very mucous forming, therefore slowing down the cleansing process.

Research indicates that the intestines in carniverous animals are shorter than those in herbiverous animals. The meat must pass through the colon quickly or it putrifies, forming toxins that are assimilated into the body. The human intestine is longer than the intestine of carniverous animals, thus indicating that the main portion of his diet should be vegetables and fruits.

If animal protein is used, red meat and pork should be used sparingly. Fish, fresh chicken and fowl are the best.

The diet should consist mainly of fresh fruits and vegetables, nuts, and seeds. Vegetables should be eaten raw whenever possible, but if they are cooked, they should be steamed just until tender, or baked.

Vitamin and mineral supplements may be added to the diet, but should be from a natural source, as some people have allergic or chemical reactions to synthetic vitamins.

If dairy products are used, soured milk products such as yogurt, cottage cheese, buttermilk and kefir are less mucous forming and should be made from fresh raw milk.

When milk is heated in pasteurization, it changes chemically and the digestive enzymes are destroyed, making it unassimable. It then creates mucous throughout the body. Raw goat's milk is easier to digest than raw cow's milk.

Butter made from raw cream is better for the body than is margarine or butter from pasteurized milk. Homemade cheese can be used on occasion, but it will cause constipation if used in excess.

All preservatives and artificial food coloring should be avoided.

FASTING

Fasting is necessary to help the body heal and throw off diseases, parasites, growths, mucous, and poisonous toxins.

There are several methods of fasting:

Mild food, juice, fruits and nuts, broth, water, or total abstinance from food and water.

We do not recommend total abstinance, nor do we recommend fasting for long periods of time without supervision from a doctor.

Studies have shown that people who fast and are deprived of their daily food intake will break down and digest their own diseased, damaged, aged, or dead cells. During this time, new, healthy cells are being produced to replace the diseased ones.

Since vitamins and minerals interfere with the cleansing process, they should be discontinued while fasting. Herbs may be used as they help to cleanse the body and regulate the glands.

Juice should be from fresh fruits and vegetables diluted with distilled water. (If these are unavailable, unsweetened canned or frozen juices may be used.) At least eight glasses of liquid should be taken during the day. The first three days are the hardest, but the most benefit comes after the third day. The fast is broken when the body experiences extreme hunger.

Each day of the fast should include:

Cleansing enema	Distilled or spring water
Dry brush massage	Herb teas
Hot and cold shower	Diluted juices
Walking or other exercise	Vegetable broth
At least a one hour rest	

Vegetable Broth

Chop or grate the following into 1½ quarts of boiling water:
  2 large red potatoes (skins included)
  3 stalks celery
  3 medium beets

4 carrots
Add any of the following vegetables: cabbage, turnips, turnip tops, beet tops, onions.
Season with any of your favorite herbs — Rosemary, Sage, Thyme, Parsley, Oregano, Basil, Cayenne.

Cover and simmer 45 minutes. When slightly cool, blend in the blender and drink warm.

Anyone can fast, but it takes a determined person to break it. It should be broken properly over a period of three to four days. Remember to eat lightly and to chew your food well.

1st day:	1 fruit for breakfast vegetable salad for lunch
2nd day:	same as 1st day only add vegetable soup for dinner 2 more fruits throughout the day
3rd day:	Add larger portions of fruit and salad. Nuts and soured milk products Baked potato or squash Bread and butter Soup
4th day:	Start back on mild food.

ENEMAS

During a fast, the eliminative organs are used extensively in order to remove the concentrated wastes. This is why it is important to take enemas. When the colon is congested, toxins are absorbed back into the system manifesting themselves as fever, earache, sore throat, headache, or any other illness.

The author does not directly or indirectly dispense medical advice or prescribe the use of herbs as a form of treatment for sickness without medical approval.

There are many types of enemas but we have used the following with excellent results:

Cayenne: Used to stimulate the liver, kidneys, spleen, and pancreas. It will also help stop bleeding.
Caution: If a person has serious problems in the colon, this could cause a burning sensation.
Add ½ teaspoon cayenne to a bag of water.

Garlic: Used for a general cleanser and to help eliminate parasites. Blend 1 or 2 garlic buds for each bag, in 1 quart of water. Strain. Add enough water to fill the bag. Do this three times.

Catnip: Use for fever, colic, and contagious diseases. It is very relaxing to the whole system.
Make a tea of 2 Tablespoons catnip in a quart of water. Strain. Add enough water to fill the bag.

Slippery Elm: Used for diarrhea, colitis, and hemorrhoids. Put 1 Tablespoon powder in blender with 1 pint of water. Add enough water to fill the bag.

White Oak Bark: Used for hemorrhoids, colitis, and it is very healing. Make a tea with 2 Tablespoons white oak bark. Add enough water to fill the bag.

When available, distilled water should be used. The knee-chest position helps the water to go through the colon better. The first bag should be warm water, as it relaxes the colon and the water is expelled faster. The second and third bags should be slightly cool water to stimulate the peristaltic action. The water is retained longer to break loose the toxins and pockets of decayed matter.

Lubricate the end of the tube with vitamin E, or petroleum jelly. Insert it just inside the rectum. As the water runs in, you can slowly insert the tube further. Never go further than 18 to 24 inches, and only as long as it moves rather easily. Don't ever force the tube in further.

The moment you have a slight cramp, or feel a need to expel, remove the tube and relax for elimination. Don't hold the water longer, as this only balloons out the colon.

101

Continue to do this until you have used 3 bags. For children, adjust this amount according to age. Always take acidophilus, yogurt, buttermilk, or kefir to replace the natural bacteria in the colon after taking enemas.

PERSPIRATION

Perspiring helps rid the body of toxins. Hot baths, and the use of certain herbs in the bath water will increase the circulation and open the pores. Any of the following may be used:

1. Add 3 to 4 Tablespoons of ginger to a tub of hot water.
2. Add 1 cup vinegar and ½ cup salt to a tub of hot water. Sit in the tub until perspiration ceases.
3. Put enough mineral water in a pan to cover the feet. Soak them for ½ hour.

Take a cool shower after each hot bath to close the pores.

To eliminate toxins faster, sip several glasses of water while in the tub.

CAUTION: Some people get dizzy while sitting in a tub of hot water so we suggest that there be some type of ventilation or a cold cloth to use on the forehead.

If a person has a fever, do not use hot water. Cool water will help bring the fever down quicker.

EXERCISE

Since illness is caused by blocked circulation, exercise is important to increase the circulation. It is usually needed the most when you feel the least like doing it.

Exercise will help move the toxins through the lymphatic system and out of the body through the colon, kidneys, skin, and eliminative organs.

In his article, "Jogging Can Kill You," Dr. J. E. Schmidt indicates that jogging can be injurious to the body as it often jars the organs and skeletal system. Jumping and running are good if they are done on some soft, or flexible surface, such as a trampoline. There are some units designed especially for this purpose already on the market. This will help the circulation and cause one to breathe deeply, which most of us fail to do.

May I quote Dr. Paavo Airola from his lecture in September 1975.

"It is better to eat junk food and exercise than to eat good food without exercising."

DRY BRUSH MASSAGE

Dirt, dust, pollution, and inactivity cause the pores to get congested. Since the skin is the largest eliminative organ of the body, if these pores get clogged, the skin will become either too dry or too oily. Brushing the body either with a body brush or loofa helps to open up the pores so the toxins can escape.

Chapter 9

HERBAL AID FOR EMERGENCIES

The author does not directly or indirectly dispense medical advice or prescribe the use of herbs as a form of treatment for sickness without medical approval. Nutritionists and other experts in the field of health and nutrition hold widely varying views. It is not the intent of the author to diagnose or prescribe. Our intent is only to offer health information to help you cooperate with your doctor in your mutual problem of building health. In the event you use this information without your doctor's approval, you are prescribing for yourself, which is your constitutional right, but the publisher assumes no responsibility.

ASTHMA
For an acute attack, put several drops of Tincture of Lobelia in the mouth and it will relax the throat. Usually the colon needs to be cleaned out to help the whole system.

BEE STINGS
Apply ice until swelling and pain are gone. Honey helps pull out the stinger and neutralizes the poison. Mud or Redmond Clay can be used if Honey is not available.

BLEEDING
Golden Seal, or Plantain applied directly on wound. Take either of above internally. If there is heavy bleeding, take cayenne in hot water until it stops. (See Hemorrhage) Cayenne can be applied externally on small wounds.

BURNS
Apply ice water and keep cloth wet and cold until pain leaves. Apply Aloe Vera on burn and also take internally. Combination (24) mixed with either Vitamin E or mineral water makes an excellent poultice. Always apply Vitamin E on burn before applying poultice. Honey applied on burn also helps.

COUGH

¼ teaspoon each of Cayenne and Ginger.

1 Tablespoon each of Honey and Vinegar.

Add 2 Tablespoons hot water, mix and take by spoon.

Mix juice from ½ lemon with 2 Tablespoons Honey and take every 15 minutes.

Licorice Root Tea or Tincture of Lobelia can be taken.

CROUP

Cleanse the Colon with a Catnip Tea Enema. A few drops of Tincture of Lobelia by mouth helps to relax. Eucalyptus Oil used in the steamer.

DIARRHEA Any of the following may be used:

½ teaspoon Nutmeg several times a day.

1 Tablespoon of Slippery Elm in bag of water as an enema.

Raspberry Leaf Tea as enema or internally.

1 teaspoon of Carob Powder in 1 cup boiled milk.

1 teaspoon whole cloves steeped in 1 quart water used as tea.

EARACHE

Take a cleansing enema to clean out the colon. Oil of Mullein or Oil of Garlic or Tincture of Lobelia in the ear. Ice pack on ear to help constrict blood vessels. B & B Tincture drops in ear. (See Directions Chapter)

FEVER

Take a Catnip Tea Enema to break loose congestion. 1,000 milligrams of Vitamin C each hour throughout the day. Juices. Tepid ginger or vinegar and salt bath.

FLU

(11) for intestinal flu.

Cleansing enema, vitamin C, juices.

Raspberry Tea, Echinacea are both good for flu.

4 Teaspoons each of Catnip and Peppermint in 1 quart boiling water. Steep and drink. Go to bed and perspire.

GALL STONES

3 Day Gall Stone Cleanse:

1st day: Apple juice all day. Before going to bed take 1 cup olive oil and ½ cup lemon juice.

2nd day: Enema in morning and then same as first day.

3rd day: Same as second day.

Alternate Cleanse: Two days of apple juice and on third

morning, take 1 cup olive oil and 1 cup lemon juice followed by a garlic enema.

When the stones are passed, they are usually a dark green or black in color.

HEMORRHOIDS

Cut a piece of raw, red potato the size of your little finger and apply vitamin E. Insert this in rectum at night. This helps take away the pain and reduce the swelling. Take a White Oak Bark tea enema — 1 Tablespoon of the herb to a bag of water.

SORE THROAT

Take an enema. Swab the throat with glycerine and iodine. Put an onion pack around the neck. (See chapter on Definitions and Directions; see also TONSILLITIS)

Wring a cloth out of strong salt water solution and put it around the neck with a plastic cover to keep the moisture in and the pillow dry.

Vitamins A, C.

TONSILLITIS

Take a garlic enema. 1,000 milligrams vitamin C every hour with 2 capsules of (17). Swab or gargle with glycerine and iodine. (Use enough iodine in the glycerine to make it a deep amber color.)

The enema cleans out the colon so the infection has a place to go, the vitamin C and (17) help to fight infection, and the glycerine and iodine help to take the swelling down.

Usually one day is sufficient, but sometimes it will take longer.

BIBLIOGRAPHY

Adams, Ruth and Frank Murray. *All You Should Know About Health Foods*. New York: Larchmont Books, 1975.

Airola, Paavo. *How To Get Well*. Phoenix, Arizona: Health Plus Publishers, 1974.

Clegg, Bud, ed. *Herbalist*, Provo, Utah: Bi-World Publishers, 1976.

Dickey, Esther. *Passport to Survival*. Salt Lake City, Utah: Bookcraft Publishers, 1969.

Griffin, LaDean. *No Side Effects*. Provo, Utah: Bi-World Publishers, 1975.

Harris, Ben Charles. *Eat the Weeds* New Canaan, Connecticut: Keats Publishing, Inc., 1973.

Hawley, Don, ed. *Life and Health National Health Journal*. Washington, D.C.: Review and Herald Publishing Association, 1973.

Hylton, William H., ed. *The Rodale Herb Book*. Emmaus, Pennsylvania: Rodale Press, 1975.

Kloss, Jethro. *Back to Eden*. Santa Barbara, California: Lifeline Books, 1975.

Kordel, Lelord. *Natural Folk Remedies*. New York: Manor Books, Inc., 1976.

Lust, John. *The Herb Book*. Sini Valley, California: Benedict Lust Publications, 1974.

Moulton, LeArta. *Nature's Medicine Chest*. Provo, Utah: The Gluten Co., 1975.

Taub, Harold J., ed. *Let's Live*. Los Angeles, California: Oxford Industries, Inc., 1976.

INDEX

18

BLOOD PRESSURE - 13, 14, 16, 19, 22, 23, 30, 31, 32, 33, **49**

BLOOD PURIFIER - 11, 12, 13, 14, 16, 17, 18, 24, 29, 31, 35, 36, **49**

BLUE COHOSH - 9, **13**, 48, 49, 52, 53, 55, 56, 58, 64, 67, 68, 70, 71, 73, 74, 76, 84, 89, 90

BLUE VERVAIN - 9

BLUEBERRIES - 56, 77

BOILS - 8, 9, 11, 13, 14, 16, 17, 18, 23, 25, 26, 28, 29, 31, 32, 35, 36, **49**

BOWELS - 14, 17, 32 **54**, 65

BRAIN - 22

BREASTS - 9, 29, 31, **50**

BRIGHAM TEA - **13**, 46, 47, 49, 53, 60, 64, 65, 70, 74, 81, 82, 83, 84

BRONCHITIS - 12, 14, 15, 16, 17, 18, 19, 20, 21, 24, 25, 29, 30, 31, 32, 33, 36, **50**

BRUISES - 17, 19, 23, 24, 25, 27, 30, 34, 36, **50**

BUCHU - **14** 47, 48, 56, 77, 80, 81, 88

BUCKTHORN - **14**, 54, 62, 63, 66, 69, 71, 78, 82, 84, 90

BURDOCK - **14**, 44, 45, 46, 47, 48, 49, 51, 52, 53, 59, 62, 63, 64, 66, 69, 70, 71, 76, 77, 79, 81, 82, 84, 85, 86, 88, 89

BURNS - 8, 9, 11, 14, 17, 21, 23, 25, 28, 32, 34, **51, 104**

BURSITIS - 11, 14, 16, 17, 24, 26, 34, 35, **51**

C

CALCIUM - 45, 46, 48, 51, 52, 53, 53, 56, 61, 64, 65, 68, 69, 71, 72, 74, 76, 77, 78, 79, 81, 82, 83, 88, 91

CALLOUS - 14, 60

CAMOMILE -**14**, 46, 47, 49, 50, 53, 54, 56, 58, 59, 60, 62, 63, 64, 65, 66, 68, 70, 73, 74, 76, 78, 84, 85, 90

CANCER - 16, 17, 18, 20, 23, 27, 29, 32, 36, **51**

CANKER - 12, 14, 17, 21, 26, 29, **51**

CAPSICUM - **15**

CAROB - **15**, 53, 57, 85

CASCARA SAGRADA - **15**, 54, 55, 56, 57, 62, 66, 68, 70, 71, 76, 84

CATARACTS - 16, 18, **52**

CATNIP - **15**, 50, 53, 54, 56, 57, 58, 60, 63, 64, 67, 68, 69, 70, 73, 74, 76, 77, 78, 84, 85, 88

CAYENNE - 9, **16**, 37, 44, 45, 46, 47, 49, 50, 51, 52, 53, 54, 55, 56, 57, 58, 59, 60, 63, 64, 65, 68, 70, 73, 74, 75, 77, 78, 79, 81, 82, 83, 84, 85, 86, 89, 90, 91

CELERY - 76

CHAPARRAL - **16**, 44, 45, 46, 47, 49, 51, 52, 55, 56, 59, 64, 70, 77, 80, 81, 82, 87, 90

CHICKEN POX - 14, 20, 21, 24, 36, **52**

CHICKWEED - **17**, 44, 45, 46, 47, 49, 50, 51, 52, 54, 56, 62, 64, 66, 69, 72, 75, 77, 79, 80, 81, 82, 84, 85, 86, 87, 88, 90

CHILDBIRTH - 13, 24, 26, 29, 33, 35, 45, **52**

CHILLS - 12, 16, 28, **52**

CHOLERA - 28

CHLORINE - 51

CIRCULATION - 16, 17, 21, 22, 23, 28, 30, 35, **52**, 102

CLEANSING - 14, 17, 18, **53, 98**

CLOVES - 47, 56, 57, 86

COLDS - 12, 14, 15, 16, 20, 21, 24, 27, 28, 29, 30, 31, 33, 35,

36, **53**
COLIC - 13, 15, 19, 27, 28, 30, 33, **53, 93**
COLITIS - 15, 17, 20, 21, 24, 25, 26, 28, 29, 32, **53**
COLON - 12, 15, 17, 20, 26, 29, 32, 33, 35, **54**, 63, 65
COMBINATIONS - 37 to 43
COMFREY - 8, **17**, 45, 46, 47, 48, 49, 50, 51, 53, 54, 55, 56, 57, 59, 60, 61, 62, 63, 64, 65, 66, 68, 69, 70, 71, 72, 73, 75, 77, 79, 81, 82, 83, 85, 86, 87, 88, 90
CONGESTION - 24, 27, 35
CONSTIPATION - 11, 13, 14, 15, 17, 18, 20, 21, 24, 25, 29, 32, 33, **54, 93**
CONTAGIOUS DISEASES - 15, 16, 20, 24, 28, 30, 33, 35, **54**
CONVULSIONS - 13, 16, 19, 21, 22, 23, 24, 25, 27, 31, 33, 34, 35, **55**
CORNS - 14, 60
CORNSILK - 47, 48
COUGH - 12, 15, 16, 17, 19, 20, 21, 22, 23, 24, 25, 26, 27, 28, 29, 30, 31, 32, 33, 34, 35, 36, **55, 105**
CRAMP BARK - 73
CRAMPS - 11, 13, 15, 16, 17, 18, 19, 20, 24, 27, 28, 32, 33, 35, 37, **55, 56**
CROUP - 15, 18, 24, 26, 33, **56, 105**
CUSHING'S DISEASE -24
CUTS - 9, 12, 16, 26, **56**
CYSTITIS - 32, 33, **56**

D
DAIRY PRODUCTS - **98**
DAMIANA -**17**, 62, 67, 71, 73, 78, 80, 82, 83
DANDELION - **18**, 44, 45, 46, 49, 50, 51, 53, 54, 55, 56, 59, 60, 62, 65, 67, 68, 69, 70, 71, 77, 81, 82, 84, 88, 89, 90
DANDRUFF - 15, 23, 31, 34, **56**
DECOCTION - **7**
DESERT TEA - **13**
DIABETES - 11, 12, 13, 14, 16, 17, 18, 19, 21, 22, 23, 24, 29, 31, 33, 35, **56**
DIAPER RASH - 26, 32, **57, 93**
DIARRHEA - 11, 12, 13, 15, 17, 20, 23, 26, 28, 29, 31, 32, 33, 35, **57, 93, 105**
DIET - **98**
DIGESTION - 11, 12, 13, 15, 16, 17, 18, 19, 21, 22, 23, 24, 27, 30, 31, 32, 33, **57**
DIURETIC - 13, 22, 23, 30, 32, **58**
DIVERTICULITIS - 15, 20, 27, 28, 29, 32, **58**
DIZZINESS - 15, 22, 28, 30, 31, 32, 35, **58**
DOG BITES -23
DOUCHE -26, **58**
DRUG WITHDRAWAL - 15, 24, **58**
DYSENTERY - 12, 29, 32, 33, **58**

E
EAR INFECTION - 8, 11, 24, 36, **58**
EARACHE - 9, 22, 24, 26, 36, 105
EARS - 36
ECHINACEA - **18**, 44, 47, 48, 49, 50, 60, 63, 65, 68, 72, 80, 84, 87, 89, 90
ECZEMA - 11, 13, 14, 17, 18, 21, 24, 32, **59**
EMERGENCIES - **104**
EMPHYSEMA - 17, 19, 20, 24, 25, 30, **59**
ENDURANCE - 14, 16, 18, 20, 21, 22, 24, 36, **59**

50, 55, 56, 63, 64, 67, 70, 72, 75, 77, 80, 85, 86, 90

K

KELP - **24**, 48, 51, 52, 53, 55, 56, 59, 63, 67, 70, 73, 74, 77, 79, 80, 81, 87

KIDNEYS - 11, 12, 13, 14, 15, 16, 17, 18, 21, 23, 24, 25, 26, 27, 28, 29, 30, 32, 33, 34, 35, 36, **70**

KIDNEY STONES - 15

L

LABOR - **70**

LACTATION - 13, 19, 25, 27, 29, 31, **70**

LARYNGITIS - 25, 31, 36, **71**

LAXATIVE - 27, 29, 32

LEG CRAMPS - **55**

LETTUCE - 76, 80

LEUCORRHEA - 12, 13, 17, 19, 21, 26, 28, 29, 32, 33, 34, **71**

LICE - **23**

LICORICE - **24**, 45, 46, 47, 49, 50, 53, 54, 58, 59, 67, 71, 72, 73, 82, 83, 85, 86, 88, 89

LIVER - 12, 14, 15, 18, 20, 21, 22, 23, 24, 25, 26, 27, 28, 29, 32, 33, 34, 35, 36, 37, **71**

LOBELIA - 8, 9, **24**, 45, 46, 47, 48, 50, 51, 53, 54, 55, 56, 57, 59, 60, 64, 67, 68, 69, 71, 72, 73, 74, 75, 76, 77, 79, 80, 81, 82, 83, 85, 86, 87, 90

LOCK JAW - 16, 24, **71**

LONGEVITY - 19, 21, 22, 24, **71**

LOW BLOOD PRESSURE - 18, 22, 27, **71**

LOW BLOOD SUGAR - **72**

LUMBAGO - 12, 23, 26, 27, 28, 29, 33, **72**

LUMPS - 8

LUNGS - 12, 13, 17, 18, 19, 21,

22, 23, 24, 25, 26, 27, 28, 31, 32, 33, 36, 37, 65, **72**

LUPUS - 13, **72**

LYMPH - 8, 18, 21, **72**

M

MAGNESIUM - 45, 46, 48, 49, 53, 56, 57, 61, 65, 67, 70, 72, 78, 81, 82

MAGNOLIA - **25**, 58, 60, 84, 89

MANDRAKE - **25,** 53, 54, 60, 62, 71, 90

MANGANESE - 48, 71

MARSHMALLOW - **25**, 45, 47, 48, 51, 55, 56, 58, 60, 61, 64, 66, 67, 69, 70, 72, 73, 75, 76, 77, 79, 86, 88, 89

MASSAGE - 103

MEASLES - 15, 21, 23, 28, 29, 30, 32, 34, 36, **73**

MEMORY - 22

MENOPAUSE - 12, 17, 22, 24, 32, **73**

MENSTRUATION - 12, 13, 14, 17, 19, 21, 22, 25, 26, 27, 28, 29, 30, 31, 32, 33, 34, 36, 55, **73**

MENTAL FATIGUE - 22

MIGRAINE HEADACHES - 13, 19, 24, 28, 30, 32, 33, 34, 35, **74**

MILK - 13, 19, 27, **74, 98**

MILKWEED - 90

MINERAL SOURCES - 11, 95, 96

MINERAL WATER - 8

MISCARRIAGE -12, 15, 19, 24, **74**

MISTLETOE - **25**, 49, 55, 62, 64, 68, 73, 76

MORMON TEA - **13**

MORNING SICKNESS - 11, 15, 20, 21, 22, 24, 27, 28, 29, 31, 34, **74**

114

SEIZURES - 23
SENILITY - 18, 22, **82**
SENNA - **32**, 54, 70, 71, 78
SEX DESIRE - 17, 22, 24, 31, 32, 35, **83**
SHEPHERD'S PURSE - **32**, 46, 49, 52, 54, 58, 61, 65, 66, 70, 72, 73, 74, 89, 90
SHINGLES - 28, 33, **83**
SHOCK - 16, 20, 25, 34, **83**
SILICA - 23
SILICON - 55
SINUS - 12, 14, 19, 20, 21, 22, 23, 26, 35, **83**
SKIN - 103
SKIN DISEASE - 12, 14, 17, 18, 21, 22, 23, 26, 27, 29, 31, 34, 36, **84**
SKUNK CABBAGE - 9
SLEEP - 27, **84**
SLIPPERY ELM - 8, 9, **32**, 46, 48, 50, 51, 53, 54, 55, 56, 57, 58, 59, 60, 61, 63, 65, 67, 69, 71, 72, 79, 83, 84, 85, 86, 87, 88, 89, 90, 91
SMOKING - 12, 15, 18, 25, 28, 31, 32, 34, **84**
SNAKE BITE - 12, 18
SORE THROAT - **84**
SORES - 8, 9, 11, 21, **84**
SPASMS - 13, 19, 28, 34
SPEARMINT - **32**, 63, 75, 85
SPIKENARD - 49, 52
SPLEEN - 12, 15, 16, 18, 21, 27, 33, 34, 36, **84**
SPRAINS - 8, 16, 17, 35, 36, **84**
SQUAW TEA - **13**
SQUAW VINE - **33**, 52, 60, 74, 76, 88
STERILITY - 19, **85**
ST. JOHNSBREAD - **15**
ST. JOHNSWORT - **33**, 45, 47, 55, 57, 63, 65, 68, 70, 72, 74, 76, 88, 91
STOMACH - 11, 12, 14, 15, 16,

17, 19, 20, 21, 23, 24, 26, 27, 28, 29, 30, 31, 32, 33, 34, 35, 56, 62, **85**
STONES - 15, 63, **85**
STRAWBERRY - **33**, 76
STRESS - 15, 22, **85**
ST. VITUS DANCE - 12, 25, **85**
SUNBURN - **85**
SUNSTROKE - 27, **85**
SWELLING - 8, 14, 15, 17, 36, **68, 85**
SYPHILLIS - **85**

T
TEETH - 11, 13, 25, 26, 34, **86**
TEETHING - 25, **93**
TENSION - 15
TETANUS - 25, **86**
THROAT - 12, 14, 16, 17, 19, 21, 23, 24, 25, 26, 29, 31, **86, 106**
THRUSH - 26, 28, 30, 34, **86**
THYME - **33**, 46, 55, 56, 57, 61, 64, 65, 68, 72, 74, 75, 76, 83, 85, 90
THYROID - 12, 21, 23, 24, 26, 27, 29, **87**
TINCTURES - **8, 9**, 13
TONGUE - **87**
TONSILLITIS - 8, 17, 18, 21, 31, 32, 34, 35, **87, 106.**
TOOTHACHES - 22, 23, 25, 26, 28, 34, 37, **87**
TOXINS - **102**
TREMORS - 29
TUBERCULOSIS - 36, **87**
TUMORS - 9, 16, 17, 25, 26, 28, 36, **87**
TURKEY RHUBARB - **33**, 54, 56
TYHPOID - **87**

U
ULCERS - 10, 11, 12, 14, 17, 19, 20, 21, 22, 23, 24, 26, 28,

116

29, 31, 32, 34, **88**
URETHRA - 14, 26
URIC ACID - 30
URINATION - 15, 19, 26, 29, 32, 33, 34, 36, 66, **88**
UTERUS - 12, 15, 19, 21, 26, 29, 32, 33, 34, 36, 66, **88**
UVA URSI - **33**, 47, 48, 50, 56, 57, 58, 66, 70, 71, 72, 73, 75, 77, 80, 84, 89

V

VAGINA - 12, 13, 16, 19, 20, 21, 25, 26, 28, 29, 32, 33, 34, 66, **89**
VALERIAN - **33**, 37, 44, 45, 49, 53, 54, 55, 57, 61, 63, 65, 67, 68, 69, 73, 74, 76, 77, 82, 83, 84, 85, 88
VARICOSE VEINS - 12, 16, 34, 35, **89**
VEGETABLE BROTH - **99**
VENEREAL DISEASE - 13, 14, 18, 21, 33, 35, 36, **89**
VERVAIN - **34**, 55, 62, 64, 73, 74, 76, 84, 91
VINEGAR - 8, 9
VITALITY - 18, 22, 24, 36, **89**
VITAMINS - 11, 94, 95
VITAMIN SOURCES - 94, 95
VOICE - 19, **89**
VOMITING - 25, **90**

W

WARTS - 14, 16, 20, 25, 26, **90**
WATER RETENTION - 19, 21, 22, 23, 27, 28, 29, 58, **90**
WEIGHT - 24
WHITE OAK BARK - **34**, 44, 49, 50, 58, 61, 62, 63, 65 66, 70, 71, 73, 75, 78, 81, 84, 86, 87, 88, 89
WHOOPING COUGH - 21, 26, 33, **90**
WILD LETTUCE -37, 77

WILD OREGON GRAPE - **11**
WILD YAM - **34**, 73, 74, 75, 77, 88
WILLOW - 13, **34**, 46, 47, 51, 55, 56, 60, 61, 62, 63, 64, 65, 82, 83, 91
WINTERGREEN - **35**, 56, 60, 61, 64, 89
WITCH HAZEL - **35**, 58, 60, 63, 66, 75, 83, 89, 91
WOOD BETONY - **35**, 47, 49, 50, 55, 57, 58, 63, 64, 65, 68, 69, 70, 73, 74, 76, 77, 78, 87, 89, 91
WORMS - 27, **90**, **93**
WORMWOOD - **35**, 45, 46, 50, 51, 52, 57, 61, 62, 63, 65, 68, 71, 78, 85
WOUNDS - 8, 9, 12, 16, 17, 18, 21, 22, 25, 26, 27, 28, 32, 33, 34, 35, 36, 56, **90**

Y

YARROW - **35** 46, 47, 49, 51, 53, 54, 56, 59, 61, 65, 66, 70, 71, 72, 73, 75, 76, 78, 79, 84, 88
YEAST INFECTION - 20, **91**
YELLOW DOCK - **36**, 41, 45, 49, 50, 51, 52, 53, 59, 60, 62, 69, 71, 77, 79, 81, 82, 84, 87, 89
YERBA SANTA - **36**, 47, 48, 49, 50, 53, 55, 61, 64, 65, 67, 69 72, 75, 82,

Z

ZINC - 55, 80, 91